WEIGHT
TRAINING

About the author

Dr. Rasch purchased his first barbell in 1926 and has been closely involved with this form of training ever since. He took an AA degree at Fullerton District College, California, where he was captain of the wrestling team and a member of Alpha Gamma Sigma honorary scholastic society. After World War II service in the Navy, from which he has since retired as a Lieutenant Commander, he attended the University of Southern California. Here he was captain of the fencing team and obtained a B.A. degree in physical education. Later he added M.A., M.Ed., and Ph.D. degrees to his academic background and was elected a member of the Phi Kappa Phi honorary scholastic society.

Since graduation from the University Dr. Rasch has worked as a corrective therapist at the Veterans Administration Hospital, Los Angeles; Director of the Biokinetics Research Laboratory, California College of Medicine, Los Angeles; and Chief, Physiology Division, Naval Medical Field Research Laboratory, Camp Lejeune, North Carolina, where he also served as physiologist for the U.S. Marine Corps Physical Fitness Academy. He is author or coauthor of several books and well over one hundred articles. Dr. Rasch is a Fellow of the American College of Sports Medicine, a member of the Research Council of the American Alliance for Health, Physical Education, and Recreation, an Honorary Life Member of the Royal Air Force School of Physical Training, and is listed in Who's Who in Science. He is now studying physical anthropology at California State University, Domingue Hills in a search for new insights into physical development.

WEIGHT TRAINING

Physical Education Activities Series

Philip J. Rasch

Formerly Chief, Physiology Division
Naval Medical Field Research Laboratory
Camp Lejeune, North Carolina

HONORARY LIFE MEMBER
Royal Air Force School of
Physical Training

THIRD EDITION

Wm C Brown Company Publishers
Dubuque, Iowa

Consulting Editors
  Physical Education
  Aileene Lockhart
  Texas Woman's University

  Parks and Recreation
  David Gray
  California State University, Long Beach

  Health
  Robert Kaplan
  The Ohio State University

Evaluation Materials Editor
  Physical Education Activities
  Jane A. Mott
  Texas Woman's University

Printed in the United States of America

6/80

Contents

Preface

The writer first took up weight training in the late 1920s in an effort to add body weight for high school football. At that time this form of exercise was still somewhat less than respectable. Coaches warned it would make one slow, was bad for the heart, and would produce other unpleasant effects in those who practiced it. This sort of idea was largely laid to rest during World War II when Thomas L. DeLorme, M.D. came out unreservedly in support of weight training and documented his claims with case histories of numerous patients. The tide quickly reversed; exercise systems that weight trainers had practiced for decades suddenly blossomed in the medical literature as the "Zinovieff" or the "Oxford" technique. The same process continues today as exercise physiologists are legitimizing Hise's theories by their studies of "elastic rebound training," with no mention whatever that weight trainers were employing these techniques half a century ago.

In the last fifteen years or so the study of what the academicians prefer to call "progressive resistance exercise" has become an accepted topic for master's theses and doctoral dissertations. Gradually we are developing a scientific basis for this form of exercise, although there is still a great deal we do not know.

It is a curious fact that those who have had the most to gain financially by promoting weight training have done the least to validate its methodology or claims. No magazine devoted to the subject and no proprietor of a weight training gymnasium has ever sponsored a research study which has increased our knowledge of exercise physiology. Nor do the great majority of those writing for such journals appear to have the slightest comprehension of the uses and importance of statistical evaluation of their claims. Consequently most of what they publish is of value only as personal anecdotes.

Both medical journals and research materials have been extensively reviewed for this edition. The contents of this text are as scientific as is possible at this point in time. Because many aspects of the subject are still controversial this material has been documented much more heavily than is customary in other publications in this series.

The most noticeable change that has occurred since the appearance of the Second Edition is the sudden upsurge in the acceptance of weight training for women. In some gymnasia men and women now train together. In part this seems due to the credit weight training has received for the success of the East German women athletes in the Montreal Olympics; American women athletes and their coaches have been forced to accept the fact that if they are going to compete on equal terms with the representatives of the East European bloc they are going to have to train as hard as do their opponents. In recognition of this development a chapter on weight training for women has been included in this edition.

A chapter on safety precautions in weight training has also been included. All other chapters have been reviewed and revised in the light of the best information now available. One thing remains unchanged: you will get out of weight training just about what you put into it.

Acknowledgments

The writer is indebted to members of the staff of the Library of California State University, Dominguez Hills for their courtesy in helping the author obtain the research materials used in the preparation of this booklet. The assistance received from David P. Willoughby is particularly and gratefully acknowledged.

Al Feuerbach. In 1974 this athlete was National AAU shot put and 242 lb. weight lifting champion. **Los Angeles Times** photo.

Introduction
to weight training

1

Prior to World War II the practice of weight training was confined largely to competitive weight lifters and to professional or amateur "strong men." Athletes in general carefully avoided the weights as their coaches and trainers solemnly warned them that their use would make a man muscle-bound, or "strain his heart," whatever this might mean. The fact that the situation is now so different resulted largely from the pioneering efforts of an Army surgeon, Thomas L. DeLorme, during World War II. Himself a weight lifter, DeLorme was instrumental in introducing the equipment and techniques of this method of training into the Army's orthopedic treatment procedures. The publication of his *Progressive Resistance Exercise* in 1951 marked the beginning of a whole new era in this form of exercise. Hellebrandt hailed his work in these words: "The recent demonstration of how much can be done to expedite the return of normal function by the systematic use of judiciously administered exercise, graded in dosage, is one of the important contributions of the period to human knowledge."[1]

Once the use of weights was approved by the medical profession, the opposition of coaches and physical educators quickly vanished. As a result, this method of training experienced a tremendous growth in public interest. Inevitably this led to specialization as users of weights sought the most efficacious methods of attaining their varied goals. Weight trainers today may be roughly divided into five groups.

Weight Lifters This group comprises competitive lifters interested mainly in acquiring the strength, speed, agility, and technique necessary to achieve success in the two Olympic lifts: the two-hand snatch and the two-hand clean and jerk. They usually employ maximal or near-maximal poundages and do not do over three repetitions of a given exercise at a time. They may perform single repetitions with rest periods between. In 1977 there were 7,477 weight lifters registered with the Amateur Athletic Union (AAU).

Power Lifters The World Power Lift Federation now recognizes thirteen nations, but the International Power Lift rules differ in some respects from the American rules. Power lifters are concerned almost exclusively with the development of brute strength. They compete in the three power lifts—squat, bench press, and dead lift, contested in that order—in which relatively large amounts of weight may be handled. On occasion the curl or some other form of lifting may be added, and the event is then billed as an Odd Lifts Meet. The training program of power lifters tends toward the use of extremely heavy weights with low repetitions and a large number of sets. During 1977 only 366 power lifters were on the rolls of the AAU.

Body Builders Physique contestants are more interested in developing massive musculature and great definition than exceptional strength. They tend to perform several sets of an exercise with a high number of repetitions in each set in an effort to engorge the muscle tissue with blood. Since the relationship between limb girth and strength is relatively small, they are not always as strong as their muscle size might lead the observer to expect. Only rarely are they outstanding athletes. A mere 177 body builders carried AAU cards in 1977.

Athletes Weight training has become extremely popular as a method of preparation for participation in athletics, particularly among weight throwers, football players, and swimmers. They practice special programs designed by their coaches to develop strength in the movements characteristic of their sport.

Patients Progressive resistance exercises under medical supervision are prescribed to meet a patient's individual needs and are often concentrated on the afflicted area rather than over the entire body. In many cases a bodybuilder routine is followed, as the restoration to normal appearance of an atrophied limb (the so-called cosmetic effect) is often of greater concern to the sufferer than is regaining normal strength.

Of the foregoing, weight lifting, power lifting, and rehabilitation procedures fall outside the scope of this book and will not be considered further. The physiologic principles discussed on the following pages are, however, as valid for those engaged in these activities as for any other group.

PHYSIOLOGIC PRINCIPLES OF WEIGHT TRAINING

The bones are in effect a system of articulated levers which are moved by the skeletal muscles. Muscles may be regarded as machines which store chemical energy and convert it to mechanical work in response to impulses conducted by the nervous system. There are approximately 434 muscles, making up about 40 to 45 percent of the body weight, but only about 75 pairs are involved in the general movements of the body. A muscle consists of a large number of cells filled with a liquid protein solution called sarcoplasm. Running through this material are elements called myofibrils. These are the units actually responsible for the process of contraction. The most popular theory is that the myofibrils contain filaments which slide past each other when a muscle contracts or elongates.

There are three types of muscular contraction, each of which has been used as the basis for training systems.

Isotonic The muscle actually shortens and moves a load, such as a barbell or dumbbell through a distance, thus accomplishing a certain amount of work. Such contractions are also said to be concentric. In practice the weight that can be handled is limited to that which can be moved through the weakest point in the range of motion of a joint.

Isokinetic exercise is a modification of isotonic exercise. It utilizes a machine which controls the speed of the movement. This prevents the dissipation of muscular energy in acceleration and provides resistance which is proportional to the input of muscular force and the alterations in skeletal levers throughout the range of motion. In simpler language, it compensates for the variations in the muscle force which can be developed at various angles of a joint and provides maximal resistance at any angle. These machines are seldom seen in gymnasia at present, but many have apparatus which is somewhat similar in principle but which does not incorporate the speed control factor. These are known as **variable resistance machines** (see fig. 4.9).

Isometric The muscle is unable to move the load, such as a fixed bar, so that apparently no joint movement takes place. The muscle does not visibly shorten, and technically no work is accomplished even though the muscle is subjected to great stress. This is known as static contraction. The value of this type of exercise has been reviewed elsewhere.[2]

Lengthening The load forces the contracted muscle to extend, as when a barbell is taken from supports and slowly lowered. This is also a form of isotonic contraction and is known as eccentric contraction in order to differentiate it from concentric movements. In practice it is utilized every time a weight is lowered in a controlled manner during isotonic exercise.

These explanations are somewhat oversimplified and are not completely accurate from the standpoint of muscle physiology. A consideration of the details would take us far astray, however, and for our purposes it is satisfactory to act as if they were correct.

Much greater amounts of weight can be handled eccentrically than can be managed concentrically. While it is possible this form of exercise has certain advantages, the difficulty is that the amount of weight which can be used requires the assistance of training partners or the use of apparatus which is heavy, is expensive, and requires a good deal of space. Another serious question is the extent to which negative exercise reproduces the movements of work or sport.[3]

The amount of force that a muscle can exert depends on the number and size of its myofibrils. It has been believed for nearly seventy years that the number of fibrils cannot be increased by exercise and that growth in muscular size (hypertrophy) results from increases in the sizes of the muscle fibers. However, recent studies have raised some question about the correctness of the belief that the number of fibrils cannot change.

When a muscle is exercised, the material enclosing the cell (sarcolemma) becomes thickened and toughened and the amount of connective tissue increases. There is also an increase in certain chemical constituents of the cell, the blood flow, and the blood pressure. The capillaries (tiny blood vessels) open and dilate, and fluid is attracted from the blood into the tissue spaces. All of this may increase the weight of the muscle by as much as 20 percent. During the rest period following exercise there will be a reduction in the muscle's size, but it will tend to remain somewhat larger than it was before exercise. If the muscle is worked regularly, there will be a permanent increase in the number of capillaries, the ability of the muscle to assimilate nutritive materials will improve, and the size and functional power of the cells will increase.

In general, biochemical studies endeavoring to explain the changes resulting in muscle from training have not been very enlightening. Recently attention has tended to center on the role of the brain and spinal cord. It has been suggested that the power of a muscle depends upon the number of motor units which the nervous system is able to excite in a muscle. Possibly some of them are more easily triggered than are others, and those hardest to arouse can perhaps be brought under voluntary control only as a result of maximal or near-maximal efforts. Strength may be more neurological and psychological than physical.

Rather obviously the foregoing changes do not appear at the same rate or to the same extent in all individuals, even when they are following identical training programs. Some individuals are what the body builders call "easy gainers" (fig. 1.1); others are "hard gainers." Some men have more fibers in a given muscle than do others, or may have muscles which others lack. Even so, these differences in response to physical activity are not fully understood. By the same token, we have not discovered all the laws underlying successful training. Exercise physiologists, however, are quite confident of the following principles:

1. Strength, endurance, and muscle size increase, within limits, in response to repetitive exercise against progressively increased resistance. This is known as the **overload principle** and requires a psychological approach

Photograph courtesy of Photographic Services, Inc.

Fig. 1.1.   Bill Trumbo. Development like this requires that a man have certain natural advantages to begin with and be an "easy gainer" in addition. Trumbo's chest measurement is about 51 inches. Despite the claims in advertisements, relatively few individuals can achieve Trumbo's result.

committed to all out efforts. The **overload principle** is the basis of all programs of weight training.

2. For each individual there is an optimal pattern for such exercises. This involves the **intensity** of the stress imposed on the muscle, the **duration** of the training periods, and the **frequency** of the workouts.

3. Of the three variables in a training program, **intensity** is the most important. There is some evidence that the amount of fatigue a muscle undergoes is important in determining the training effect.

4. The critical factor is the amount of stress placed upon the body during the given training time.

5. Exercises which do not involve overloading the body systems have relatively little effect upon performance ability.

6. Muscles forced to perform repeated contractions at progressively increased loads respond by hypertrophying as well as by increasing their strength, but the relationship between hypertrophy and strength is not clear.

7. Different muscles may respond better to different programs of exercise.

8. As muscular strength increases, **trainability** (ability to respond to repeated contractions of a given force, duration, and frequency by the development of greater strength) decreases.

9. Muscles contain two types of fibers: slow twitch and fast twitch. The ratio between the two is a hereditary matter and cannot be altered by training. The top competitors in each sport have a "mix" which is especially suited to that particular activity. To this extent champion athletes are born, not made.

We do not know as much as we should like to about the best methods of invoking the overload principle, but the physiologists have several hints to offer the weight trainer.

1. A muscle is in position to exert its greatest force when it is somewhat stretched. Each movement should begin from a position in which the joint is fully extended and end with it fully contracted.
2. Mechanical efficiency is greatest at about one-fifth of the maximal speed. The movements should be made slowly and steadily, with the final position held firmly for a few seconds.
3. To permit repetitions the resistance must be sufficiently large to demand a greater-than-normal effort but small enough to require a less-than-maximal effort.
4. There is some evidence that exercise is more effective if done to a definite rhythm.
5. Short, frequent rest pauses should be observed to prevent the muscle from becoming fatigued early in the training session. This gives the heart a chance to drive blood through the muscle, rinsing out waste products and bringing in food and oxygen. The result is a greater work output even though less time is spent in actually moving the weights. In a normal training routine the optimal length of these rest pauses appears to be about three minutes.[4]

The serious weight trainer should be alert for three possible developments in his field:

1. Since different muscles may respond better to different programs of exercise, we may see the development of separate routines for various body parts.
2. Future training programs may contain rapid movements directed at stimulating fast twitch fibers and slow, prolonged movements directed at stimulation of the slow twitch fibers.
3. The validity of the second principle is not beyond question. There is evidence that mechanical efficiency is greater when flexion of a muscle is immediately followed by its extension. This is termed "elastic rebound." It is possible that rebound methods deserve more attention than they have received in weight training.

Weight trainers majoring in physical education should have no difficulty in finding research projects for their masters' theses during the next few years!

SLEEP AND NUTRITION

It seems almost unnecessary to mention that an adequate amount of sleep is necessary if a person is to profit from a training program. It is generally agreed that for the average individual this entails about eight hours a night. The time of day at which one exercises has no known effect on the results, but the weight trainer may find it difficult to get to sleep if he takes a vigorous workout just before going to bed. A man should allow an hour or so for the body systems to return to normal before he retires.

Body builders in particular have a tendency to be faddish in their diet and to consume great quantities of "health foods," "organically grown foods,"* proteins, vitamins, and other dietary supplements. As Kenneth L. Milstead, of the Federal Food and Drug Administration, has remarked, "More people seem to believe more bunk about food and nutrition than any other single topic in the health field and perhaps in any other field."[5] It is, of course, greatly to the financial advantage of those selling such products to promote belief in the need for them—a point which should be kept in mind when reading the magazines devoted to weight training.

Make a list of the dietary practices you have heard advocated for weight training or body building. Check the list against the fads and myths described in this chapter. What evidence is given for debunking the dietary practices that are useless or harmful?

Nutritionists now recommend that the daily diet be based on the Basic Four Plan:

1. Milk and milk products (two or more servings a day)
2. Meat, fish, and eggs (two or more servings a day)
3. Fruits and vegetables (four or more servings a day)
4. Breads and cereals (four or more servings a day)

The food intake of Olympic weight lifters averages around 3900 kilocalories per day. This amount should be more than ample unless the weight trainer is on a massive program to increase body weight. The major portion should be carbohydrate, as it is from this source that the body derives most of its energy. Fats also serve as an important source of energy but work efficiency is lower on a high-fat diet than on a high-carbohydrate intake. Protein is necessary for maintenance and growth of the tissues, and in this country the average diet appears to be more than adequate in this respect.

If one enjoys drinking milk and it is tolerated well, it is an excellent source of protein and other nutrients. However, a high percentage of our population finds it gives them flatulence, cramps, and diarrhea, facts which are carefully avoided by Mark Spitz when he proclaims "Milk has something for everybody." The percentage of those who cannot use milk is especially high among those of American Indian, Oriental, African, and Greek derivation. It seems to be related to the fact that their ancestors did not use

---

*Nutrition experts assert that food grown organically, that is from soil on which no chemical fertilizer or pesticide has been used, has no more nutritional value than does any other, and that in any event the quantity so grown is less than 25 percent of that sold in "organic" stores!

milk and failed to develop an enzyme called lactase which is necessary for its digestion. If one's body does not tolerate milk this should cause no worry. Simply do not drink it.

American weight trainers are notorious for the huge amounts of proteins and amino acid supplements which they ingest. Independent investigators have again and again found that no benefit results from the use of protein supplements[6, 7, 8, 9] or excess vitamins[10, 11] when the subjects are subsisting on a normal American diet. The concept that the athlete must continually replace proteins in his body has, in the words of Mayer, "been refuted again and again throughout the last hundred years."[12] As this is written the Federal Trade Commission is considering a Trade Regulation Rule which would prohibit any representation that "Use of a protein supplement can improve or increase the level of performance of athletics or strenuous physical labor by increasing strength, endurance, vitality, vigor or muscle tissue. . . ."[13] One problem is that protein is composed of amino acids. These are converted to urea and excreted in the urine. This requires water and may aggravate the dehydration commonly seen in athletes "making weight." Additionally, too much protein in the diet may leave an acid residue which imposes an extra load on the kidneys.

There are no miracle foods. Yogurt, blackstrap molasses, brewer's yeast, and similar substances are wholesome and nutritious, but no more so than other products which are usually much less expensive. There is no foundation for the claim that soil depletion causes malnutrition.

Vitamins

Vitamins are primarily regulators of biochemical functions. They do not contribute significantly to body structure and are not a direct source of energy. The athlete's need for vitamins is no greater than that of the non-athlete. If the weight trainer is ingesting a typical American diet, vitamin supplementation is probably useless and certainly costly. Cooper remarks that "Americans excrete the most expensive urine in the world because it is loaded with so many vitamins!"[14]

Massive doses of vitamins A, D, M, and the methyl group have been shown to be harmful. The reason that Central European athletes respond favorably to an increased vitamin intake is simply that their diet is normally deficient in certain of these chemicals.

It is possible, however, that athletes such as jockeys, boxers, and wrestlers who must stay on a low-calorie diet in order to "make weight" or who must train very strenuously for competition may require more vitamins than they can obtain in their normal dietary intake. What all of this seems to add up to is that if a person lives in a rooming house and gets poorly balanced meals at some local "greasy spoon" or is "making weight" for competition, vitamin-mineral supplementation of his food intake may be profitable. A properly balanced diet is the basis of good nutrition. If one wants to experiment by taking dietary additives, he is certainly privileged to do so. It is his money. He should be careful not to delude himself, however, by attributing to them results which would have been achieved without them.

Drugs

Unquestionably the greatest problem in the field of weight training today is the widespread use of anabolic steroids, the so-called tissue-building drugs. These are synthetic compounds which replicate natural hormones produced in the body and are believed to promote muscular growth. They are sometimes prescribed by physicians to treat metabolic problems which result in reduced ability to assimilate protein. Unfortunately, they may also have highly undesirable side effects. Liver damage, endocrine disturbances, testicular atrophy, and impotency in males have been reported to result from their use. Recent evidence implicates several androgenic-anabolic steroids as causes of cancer of the liver. One of them is Dianabol,[15] a drug which has been extensively used by weight trainers.

Such organizations as the International Olympic Committee and the AAU disbar any athlete or physique contestant known to have used drugs. During the Montreal Olympic Games eight weight lifters were disqualified for this reason. Nevertheless, there are persistent rumors that use of these drugs is part of the training program of the East German athletes. It is also said to be common among American body builders, football players, field athletes, and wrestlers.

Is the position of this elbow joint appropriate for beginning an exercise movement? Would it be correct if the elbow were flexed at a right angle? At about what speed of movement is mechanical efficiency greatest?

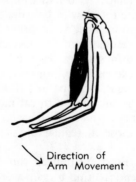

Direction of
Arm Movement

The results of research studies have been conflicting, one problem being the number of different drugs which have been used. The evidence is further confused by the fact that some steroid users report that steroids are effective only when accompanied by strenuous training, which may in itself account for some or all of the improvements observed by some users. In view of their doubtful value, the fact that users are debarred from reputable competitions, and the possibility of liver damage and other undesirable side effects, weight trainers should leave anabolic steroids strictly alone.

Alcohol and Tobacco

There is no evidence that moderate consumption of alcohol has any deleterious effect on the development of strength and hypertrophy. Tobacco is somewhat more controversial, especially so far as endurance training is concerned. While there is little in the way of direct evidence that its use is harmful to the weight trainer, the high probability that it is implicated in the development of lung cancer should in itself be enough to discourage its use.

WEIGHT NORMALIZING

The traditional prescription for normalizing the weight is that those wishing to reduce should use low resistance and high repetitions; those seeking to gain should use high resistance and low repetitions. The use of progressive resistance exercises to reduce weight is not very successful unless rigid control of the dietary intake is also instituted. Obese individuals have been found to lose some fat as a result of weight training, but there was very little change in total body weight. On the other hand, people who go on a strict diet only may lose muscle tone together with body weight. A combination of increased exercise and decreased food intake appears to be the answer. The addition of running to the training program is usually recommended. The diet should be carefully planned to make sure that it contains sufficient vitamins and minerals while remaining relatively low in calories, but there appears to be no particular advantages to either low-carbohydrate or low-fat diets. Massage, sweat baths, and the like, are of little value other than as a temporary palliative. The second, at least, results merely in loss of water, which is promptly replaced when the person drinks a few glassfuls.

Progressive resistance exercises are, however, more successful when used as an aid in putting on weight, perhaps in part because the exercise makes the subject hungry and he is encouraged to eat more. Salavantis[16] found that over a period of one semester high school boys on a weight training program gained 7.8 pounds, while those in regular physical education classes gained only 4.6 pounds.

About 1930 Mark H. Berry introduced the idea of concentrating on a few heavy exercises when endeavoring to gain weight: squats, bent arm pullovers, dead lifts, supine presses, and two-arm presses, for example. This is now an accepted procedure among weight trainers. Vern Weaver, Mr. America 1963, used only five exercises when trying to increase his body weight: decline presses, high pull-ups, parallel squats, wide grip chins, and straight-arm pull-downs. He used five or six sets of the same number of repetitions, employing as much weight as possible. These programs put on weight but do not by themselves produce attractive physiques. Their proponents insist that the proper way to attain maximum development and shapeliness is to "bulk up, train down."

MYTHS ABOUT WEIGHT TRAINING

The term "muscle bound" refers to a limitation of motion which occasionally results when a movement requiring less than the normal range of motion is constantly practiced. Bicycle riders sometimes become muscle-bound in the legs, with the result that they cannot extend the lower leg properly when trying to kick a football. Such restriction of movement is evidence of an improper training program. It is, however, true that the sheer bulk of muscle may reduce the range of a given movement and that muscular men in general have less joint mobility than do slender types. Further, each type of athletics tends to reflect a flexibility pattern peculiar to itself. Thus swimmers may exceed weight trainers in the flexibility of certain joints but be exceeded in others by the weight trainers. Apparently ranges of movement tend to become fixed within limits producing the best performance in the activity involved.

There is no evidence that practice of a proper weight-training program will make a person slow or adversely affect coordination. If anything, the opposite is true, but there seems to be a limit after which further increases in strength are not accompanied by improvement in speed.

One of the most venerable myths about weight training is that it is "bad for your heart," in what way it is bad never being explained. This fable should have been laid to rest in 1959, when Etzenhouser and his colleagues[17] examined twenty-six weight lifters and found their hearts were all within normal physiological limits. It still crops up occasionally, but subsequent studies right down to the quite recent[18] support the findings of Etzenhouser et al.

WEIGHT TRAINING AND PHYSICAL FITNESS

Having said this much it must be added the fact that weight training is unequaled as a means of developing strength does not mean it is a perfect exercise. A number of studies have shown that its practice results in very little improvement in cardiorespiratory function.[19] In tests of work capacity, weight lifters have been found to be no better than the untrained. If the weight trainer desires to be fit as well as strong, it will be necessary to add a good deal of running to the regimen—perhaps something on the order of Cooper's aerobic program.[20] In any event the activity must be vigorous enough so that the heart rate for healthy young men exceeds 150 beats per minute, or no training effect will result.

REFERENCES

1. F. A. Hellebrandt. "Recent Advances in Methods of Hastening Convalescence Through Exercise," *Southern Medical Journal*, 39:397-401, May 1946.
2. Philip J. Rasch. "Isometric Exercise and Gains of Muscle Strength." In Roy J. Shephard, ed., *Frontiers of Fitness*. Springfield, Ill.: Charles C Thomas, 1971, pp. 98-111.
3. Philip J. Rasch. "The Present Status of Negative (Eccentric) Exercise: A Review." *American Corrective Therapy Journal*, 28:77-et seq., May-June, 1974.
4. H. Harrison Clarke, et al. "Strength Decrements of Elbow Flexor Muscles Following Exhaustive Exercise, *Archives of Physical Medicine and Rehabilitation*, 35:560-561, September 1954.
5. Quoted in Charlotte (N.C.) *Observer*, 11 November 1964.
6. Philip J. Rasch and William R. Pierson. "The Effect of a Protein Dietary Supplement on Muscular Strength and Hypertrophy," *American Journal of Clinical Nutrition*, 11:530-532, November 1962.
7. Philip J. Rasch et al. "Protein Dietary Supplementation and Physical Performance," *Medicine and Science in Sports*, 1:195-199, December 1969.
8. Richard W. Cuddihee. "The Effects of Protein on Body Weight and Muscular Strength of Beginning Weight Lifters," Unpublished Master's Thesis, Springfield College, 1973.
9. Lawrence A. Golding, et al. "Weight, Size, and Strength—Unchanged with Steroids," *Physician and Sports Medicine*, 2:39-43, June 1974.
10. Philip J. Rasch, et al. "Effect of Vitamin C Supplementation on Cross Country Runners," *Sportartzliche Praxis*, 5:10-13, 1962.
11. Jean Mayer and Beverly Bullen. "Nutrition and Athletic Performance," *Physiological Reviews*, 40:369-397, July 1962.
12. Jean Mayer. "Food Fads for Athletes," *Atlantic Monthly*, 208:50-53, December, 1961.
13. *Federal Register*, September 5, 1975-40 F.R. 41144.
14. Donald L. Cooper. "Drugs and the Athlete," *Journal of the American Medical Association*, 221:1007-1011, August 28, 1972.
15. F. Leonard Johnson, et al. "Association of Androgenic-Anabolic Steroid Therapy with Development of Hepatocellular Carcinoma," *Lancet*, 2:1273-1276, December 16, 1972.
16. Salavantis, John E. "A Comparison of Body Weight Gain of a Group in a Weight Training Program Compared to a Group in a Physical Education Class Without a Weight Training Program," Unpublished Master's Report, Kansas State University, 1972.
17. Etzenhouser, Russell. "Electrocardiograms of Weight Lifters," *Journal of the Kansas Medical Society*, 60:121-125, March, 1959.
18. T. Corser, et al. "Cardiac and other muscular responses to heavy weight lifting," *Journal of Physiology*, 19:66P-67P, September, 1968.
19. Keul, J., et al. The effect of weight lifting exercise on heart rate and metabolism in experienced weight lifters. *Medicine and Science in Sports*, 10:13-15, Spring, 1978.
20. Kenneth H. Cooper, *the aerobics way*. New York: M. Evans and Company, 1977.

Safety precautions
in weight training

2

Some years ago Karpovich[1] made a detailed study of the real and alleged hazards of weight training. He found it to be one of the safest of all forms of physical activity. There were, it is true, the usual quota of strains and sprains that must be expected from any form of vigorous exercise, but they were neither exceptionally frequent nor unusually severe when compared with those resulting from other sports. The incidence of hernia and hemorrhoids were much smaller than in the normal male population of the United States, and no cases of damaged hearts were reported. Whether herniae can be prevented by developing the abdominal musculature is a highly controversial question. Some doctors believe that abdominal hernia is evidence of a defect in the muscle structure and that such defects cannot be corrected by exercise. Only four or five fatalities have been attributed to weight training; all occurred when the weight fell on a man doing supine presses.

SAFETY PRECAUTIONS

Medical authorities[2, 3] have analyzed injuries incurred by weight trainers and recommend the following safety precautions be observed:

1. Avoid training alone if at all possible.
2. Keep the weight close to the body when lifting.
3. Use correct techniques in all exercises.
4. Do not lift a weight from the floor when you are in a stooping position.
5. Avoid exaggerated "lean back" when pressing a weight overhead.
6. Avoid "hollowing" the lower back when holding a weight overhead.

Blackouts

A person pressing a heavy weight has a distinct tendency to hold his breath. The weight tends to compress the chest, and a high intrathoracic pressure is produced. There is a sudden rise in blood pressure which prevents the return of the venous blood to the heart. This causes an equally sudden drop in blood pressure, and the lifter may become dizzy and feel that he is going to faint. This is known to exercise physiologists as the Valsalva phenomenon (Valsalva was a seventeenth-century Italian anatomist) and may be deliberately used by wrestlers in such holds as the bear hug. A lifter will say that he grayed out or blacked out.

A second danger is that the Valsalva maneuver may increase intraabdominal pressure to such an extent that an inguinal hernia could be produced if there was a preexisting weakness in that area. These considerations suggest that breathing squats may be potentially dangerous to some individuals and are best omitted from the program.

Compton and associates[4] offer three suggestions to prevent blackouts:

1. Avoid hyperventilation before the lift.
2. Stay in the squatting position as short a time as possible.
3. Raise the weight as rapidly as possible to a position where normal breathing can be resumed.

Precisely because blackouts do occur, many writers on weight training stress detailed instructions in proper breathing. Unfortunately, their advice is frequently contradictory, and Karpovich and Sinning maintain that attempts at "respiratory control in athletics are mostly fanciful but futile attempts to interfere with a wonderfully adjusted breathing mechanism."[5] The general rule is to inhale while contracting the muscles and exhale as they relax.

As in any other form of activity, overtraining, i.e., exercising to the point of chronic fatigue, will reduce both performance capacity and the body's ability to resist infection.

Most men and women will profit from weight training. There are, however, certain conditions in which it is contraindicated. Those suffering from hernia, high blood pressure, fever, infection, recent surgery, or heart disease should avoid it. It is not possible to "sweat out" a cold, and there is a great deal of evidence that vigorous activity during a period of infection serves to spread throughout the body organisms which might otherwise have been sealed off and rendered relatively harmless. The result may be serious, if not fatal. Similarly, trying to hasten the metabolism of alcohol by exercising is useless and may be dangerous.

Warm up

Most weight trainers warm up with a series of calisthenic exercises, giving particular attention to stretching the back muscles. It has not been proven that warm-up is of any value in the prevention of injury and some investigators seriously question whether it has any value for this purpose. In any event there is evidence that sudden bursts of high intensity exercise without prior warm up result in changes in the electrocardiogram attributable to an inadequate oxygen supply to the heart.

Examine this drawing. What safety precautions are being violated? What corrections should be made?

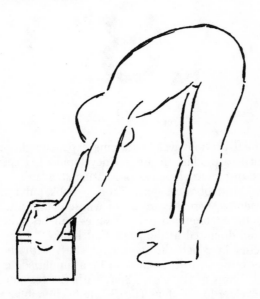

The exerciser should be careful to keep the body warm during the work out, especially when taking rest pauses. The use of a sweat shirt and sweat pants is highly recommended if the exercise area is not comfortably warm. A temperature of about 68 degrees F. or a little warmer is generally preferred.

REFERENCES

1. Peter V. Karpovich. "Incidence of Injuries in Weight Lifting." *Iron Man,* 11-7 *et seq.,* September-October, 1951. See also *Iron Man,* 26-47, August-September-October, 1967 and Los Angeles *Times* September 28, 1975.
2. J. D. G. Troup. "The Risk of Weight-Training and Weight-Lifting in Young People," *British Journal of Sports Medicine,* 5:27-33, 1970.
3. Frederick E. Jackson, *et al.* "Weight Lifting Injuries," *Journal of the American College Health Association,* 19:187-189, February, 1974.
4. D. Compton, *et al.* "Weight-Lifters' Blackout," Lancet, 2:1234-1237, 1 December 1973.
5. Peter V. Karpovich and Wayne E. Sinning. *Physiology of Muscular Activity,* 7th ed. Philadelphia: W. B. Saunders Co., 1970, p. 150.

Basic
weight training program

3

The person without previous weight training experience begins by following a routine designed to produce all-around development. Experience over the years has resulted in the development of a rather standardized set of exercises for this purpose. Most of these derive from a book published in Germany in 1907 by Theodor Siebert. Regardless of whose course one takes or whose book is bought, the recommended basic series will be quite similar to the exercises listed and discussed in the pages that follow.

In all exercises in which the movement starts with the weight at the chest, the trainer brings it to that position by a simplified version of what is known to weight lifters as the *clean*. Start with the feet on line, the knees bent, and the bar close to the shins (fig. 3.1, left). Forcibly extend the knees and pull the bar as nearly straight upward as is possible, taking a short step forward if necessary to bring the bar onto the upper part of the chest (fig. 3.1, right). The weights should be loose enough on the bar so that they will rotate freely as the arms are snapped under the bar for presses or as the bar rises toward the chest in curling. If they are not, the exerciser will develop sore wrists.

Other than a barbell, the only piece of equipment required for the following exercises is a bench. If the lifter builds his own, it should be not over eleven inches wide, of sturdy construction, and with a wide base which will prevent tipping.

BASIC PROGRAM

Two-Arms Standing Press

The bar is taken to the chest as described, pushed to arm's length overhead, and then lowered to the chest (fig. 3.2). As it passes the head, the weight

Photographs by Gene Mozee

Fig. 3.1. Modified Barbell Clean. **Left,** Proper position for lifting a weight to the chest. Note that the feet are in line with bar, not one foot forward and one back. This subject has his thumb over the bar. Most men prefer to lift it to the chest with the thumb under the bar and make the change before starting the press. **Right,** the weight is started upward by forceful extension of the knees. The lifter steps forward and under the bar as the weight is snapped onto the top of his chest, and his elbows whip under it.

Fig. 3.2. Two Arms Standing Press.

should move backward a little so that it is in line with the line of gravity of the body. Too far forward or too far backward and control of it will be lost. No spring should be imparted by flexing and straightening the knees (termed a *hitch* by weight trainers), and the exerciser should not lean backward. Most experienced lifters prefer to have the thumbs under the bar and alongside the index fingers while pressing. The press develops the shoulders and the arm extensors: triceps, deltoids, upper part of the trapezius, serratus anterior, and associated muscle groups.

High Pull-Up

The bar is held against the front of the thighs, palms in. It is then pulled up to the chin, the elbows raised as high as possible, and lowered to the starting

Fig. 3.3. Two-Arms High Pull-up.

position (fig. 3.3). The high pull-up develops the shoulders and the arm flexors: trapezius, deltoids, biceps, radialis, brachioradialis, and associated muscle groups.

Two-Arms Curl (Front Curl)

The bar is held against the front of the thighs, palms out. The elbows are kept close to the sides, and the weight is alternately brought up to the chest and lowered to the starting position (fig. 3.4). The tendency to permit the elbows to move backward or to heave the weight up by bending backward at the waist must be avoided. The exercise can be made in strict form by placing the back against the wall or a post. The bar should be lowered slowly and under full control to take advantage of exercising during the eccentric contraction phase of the movement. It is important to fully extend the elbows

Fig. 3.4.   Two-Arms Curl.

at the conclusion of this part of the exercise. The two-arms curl develops the arm flexors: biceps, radialis, brachioradialis, and associated muscle groups.

Reverse Curl

This exercise is performed in a manner similar to the foregoing, with the exception that the palms are turned in instead of out (fig. 3.5). It develops much the same muscles as the regular curl, but the exerciser will be able to handle only about two-thirds as much weight due to a change in the mechanical advantage of one of the elbow flexors.

Fig. 3.5.   Reverse Curl.

Some body builders have machine shops bend special curling bars for them. These provide vertical sections for gripping so that curls may be performed with the hands in the intermediate as well as in the front and reverse positions.

Half-Squat (Parallel Squat)

The bar is brought up to the chest in the usual manner. The knees are first flexed somewhat and then strongly extended. Simultaneously the arms are straightened so that the barbell is hurled above the head. It is then carefully lowered to rest on the shoulders behind the head. There is likely to be an uncomfortable pressure against the vertebrae, and the bars are frequently wrapped in the center with towels or other soft material or bent so as to remove this pressure. The man squats until his thighs are parallel to the floor, keeping his heels on the ground, and then rises, fully straightening the knees (fig. 3.6). The back must be kept as straight as possible, not permitted to round.

Some individuals will find that their quadriceps and hamstrings (semitendinosus and semimembranosus) are so tight that they cannot keep their heels on the floor. This forces them into a deep knee bend, with the consequent danger of falling forward. To obviate this a two-by-four-inch plank or a thick barbell plate may be placed under the heels, allowing the lifter to shift his weight backward. The deep knee bend places a little different stress on the quadriceps than does the squat, and some body builders perform both exercises for developmental purposes.

The center of gravity and the gravity line of the body shift according to the distribution of weight. Analyze several barbell exercises in terms of the adjustments required to maintain stability.

Fig. 3.6. Half-squat.

Advanced exercisers sometimes do squats with the barbell held at the collar bones (**front squats**). The back must be kept straight and the head up, or the lifter will lose his balance. The exercise is said to be excellent for the development of the thigh just above the knees, but many experienced individuals dislike it because breathing becomes difficult. Considerably less weight can be handled in front squats than in regular squats.

Before very long a lifter will reach the point at which more weight is used for the squats than can be lifted overhead. At that time a pair of adjustable squat racks or standards becomes invaluable (fig. 3.7). These are set at a height low enough so that the bar will clear the horns when the trainer

Photograph courtesy of York Barbell Company

Fig. 3.7.   Vern Weaver, Mr. America 1963, Using Adjustable Squat Racks.

stands up with the weight on his shoulders. After assuming the erect position, he takes two steps backward, performs his exercises, and then steps forward and replaces the bar, looking first to one side and then to the other to make certain that it is in proper position before bending his knees and stepping out from under it.

As originally popularized by Joseph Curtis Hise and Mark H. Berry, this exercise involved a full squat. Full squats and full deep knee bends have since been condemned by the National Federation of State High School Athletic Associations and the Committee on the Medical Aspects of Sports of the American Medical Association as potentially dangerous to the internal and supporting structures of the knee joint. It is reported, however, that some professional football teams still use the complete movement. During the forty-odd years that he has been interested in weight training, the writer has never known a man with damaged knees which were attributed to doing full squats or deep knee bends. He has, however, seen a large number of aching backs, particularly when the exerciser has permitted his spine to round to the point that the buttocks were the first part of the body to rise. While there is little experimental evidence to justify avoiding complete knee flexion, there are theoretical kinesiological reasons for hesitating to assume this position. Until the question has been clarified, it seems safer to avoid full squats and deep knee bends. A simple way of gauging the degree of knee flexion is to squat until you are sitting on a bench and then rise again.

Hise and Berry also advocated what they called "**breathing squats.**" The lifter placed the weight on the shoulders, took three to six deep breaths, held the last one, and did a single rapid squat, bouncing up from the deep position, and repeated ths procedure for as many repetitions as desired. This procedure is still advocated by some authors, but there are two serious objections to its use: in the first place, bouncing squats are considered to be a cause of knee injuries; in the second place, holding the breath while squatting may induce the **Valsalva maneuver,** which is also undesirable (see p. 14).

Squatting movements develop the knee extensors: quadriceps femoris (rectus femoris, vastus lateralis, vastus intermedius, and vastus medialis).

Heel Raises

Following completion of his squats, the lifter retains the weight on his shoulders and raises the heels as high off the ground as is possible (fig. 3.8). He then returns to the starting position. To exercise the involved muscles from several angles, one-third of the repetitions are done with the toes turned out as far as possible, one-third with the toes pointed forward, and one-third with the toes turned in. To increase the resistance, the exerciser may place the toes on the board or plates mentioned, thus increasing the range through which the calf muscles must contract. A popular alternative is to perform the exercise while seated on the bench with the weight resting on the tops of the knees. Most individuals find it necessary to place some sort of padding under the bar. A more advanced approach is to walk up and down a flight of stairs, stepping flat-footed on each tread and raising up on the toes to step onto the next one. Any way it is done, this exercise develops the foot extensors: gastrocnemius, soleus, and associated muscle groups.

Fig. 3.8.   Heel Raises.

Bent Arm Pull-Over

The exerciser lies supine on the bench, the head at one end, knees bent so that the feet are on the bench, and the entire back in contact with it. Some swaybacked individuals may not be able to achieve this. The weight is held at the chest with the elbows bent. Keeping the elbows in this position, the arms pivot at the shoulders so that the weight is swung past the head, just brushing the hair, and lowered as far as possible without causing the back to lose contact with the bench. No arching of the back is permitted at any stage of the exercise (fig. 3.9). The weight is then returned to the starting position. The elbows must be kept in, not permitted to swing out to the sides. The exercise may also be done with the reverse grip.

Fig. 3.9. Bent Arm Pull-Overs.

Pull-overs are sometimes performed with the elbows straight instead of bent, in which case considerably less weight is used. This method is not recommended since sooner or later the exerciser will use too much poundage and suffer deltoid strain or an overstretch of the elbow joint capsule. If no bench is available, the exercise can be performed on the floor, but with reduced effect. It develops the upper of the chest and back: deltoids, pectoralis, latissimus dorsi, teres major, and associated muscle groups.

Straight-Legged Dead Lift (Derrick Lift)

Bend over at the waist and pick the bar up with the alternate grip, that is, one hand facing in and one facing out. This reduces the likelihood that a heavy weight will pull the fingers open as the gripping muscles tire. The exerciser rises to the erect position and contracts the muscles of the upper back as though trying to pull the shoulder blades together. The lifter then bends over again, lowering the weight to not less than two inches from the floor (fig. 3.10). Some experienced trainers stand on a platform and lower the weight until the bar is at ankle level. It is extremely inadvisable for the novice to try this. When the body is fully flexed, the strain is borne by the ligaments of the back, with little or no assistance from the muscles. Direct injury may result, or the ligaments may be stretched and predisposed

Fig. 3.10.   Straight-Legged Dead Lift.

to further trauma. Because of the weight there is a tendency for the heels to rise off the ground. This must be resisted, or the lifter may end up by falling forward. Blocks may be utilized between the plates and the floor so that the lifter's spine is never fully flexed.

At this point a word of explanation is required. The straight-legged dead lift is simply and solely an exercise for the back muscles. When lifters talk about dead lifting, they refer to a movement in which they bend the knees and lift the weight by contracting the quadriceps. The training routine for this may include the **Hack lift**, which is a squat with the weight held behind the body, as in figure 3.17, instead of placed on the shoulders, and the straddle lift (**Jefferson and Kennedy lift**) in which the lifter straddles a barbell, one foot forward and one back, and lifts it by straightening the knees. These are actually variations of the squat and would have been included under the discussion of that exercise if it had not been necessary to clarify the fact that there are two distinct styles of dead lifting. The same precautions should be observed for the Hack lift and the straddle lift as with squatting: that is, the squat should be made to only the parallel position. The straight-legged dead lift develops the extensors of the back and hip: erector spinae, gluteus maximus, semitendinosus, semimembranosus, and related muscle groups. The Hack and straddle lifts develop primarily the quadriceps.

A variation of the straight-legged dead lift is the "**good morning exercise**" in which the barbell is placed on the shoulders in back of the neck and the exerciser first bends forward and then to each side. Only light weights should be used, and no attempt should be made to fully flex the trunk.

Another excellent exercise for developing the back muscles is the so-called **swan exercise** in which a man lies face downward and then extends his torso. This is shown in figure 4.1. In advanced training a weight may be held behind the head. The main difficulty is finding some way to securely anchor the feet.

Bench Press (Supine Press)

The exerciser lies on his back on a bench with the weight at his chest. The bar is pushed to arm's length and then lowered to the chest (fig. 3.11). It must come to a rest so that it is not bounced up off the chest.

Certain precautions should be taken during this exercise. If the weight gets off to one side, it may cause the bench to tip. For this reason the feet should be placed on the floor in a good position to resist any tendency of the

Fig. 3.11.   Bench Press. Note that the thumbs are under the bar.

bench to tip. The head should be at the end of the bench so that the weight can be dropped to the floor behind it if it tends to get away from the lifter.

If the supine press is done on the floor, the use of extralarge plates will enable the lifter to roll the weight over his head to the starting position and will protect him if his arms cannot support the wieght. If the exercise is performed on a bench, it is strongly recommended that the barbell be placed on some form of supports from which it can be lifted to start the exercise and to which it can be returned upon completion of the presses. Some of the commercially built benches have standards as an integral part of the bench (fig. 3.12), which is a great convenience.

When lifting alone without the use of standards, the exerciser may experience difficulty in getting a heavy weight into pressing position. The writer usually pulls the bar hip high, straddles the bench, sits down at the proper spot, lies back, and uses an extension of the knees and toes to heave the bar up to the chest. After the last press it is placed on the upper thighs, he sits up, and then stands with the weight. Men employing heavy weights in this exercise should practice it only when there is a partner available to assist them if they get into difficulties.

The position of the hands may be varied from close together to wide apart in order to work the muscles from different angles. The bench press develops the extensors of the arms, the shoulders, and the chest: triceps, deltoids, and pectoralis major, together with associated muscle groups.

Fig. 3.12.   Supine Bench with Integral Standards.

Press Off the Back of the Neck (POBN)

The barbell is placed on the shoulders behind the neck, as for the squat. The exercise may be done standing, which enables you to use a little more weight, but it is usual for the lifter to straddle the bench and sit down. The weight is pressed to arm's length overhead and then lowered to the shoulders behind the neck (fig. 3.13). The head must be kept slightly forward to avoid being hit by the bar as it goes up and down. It is essential that the bar not

Fig. 3.13.   Seated Press Off the Back of the Neck.

be dropped on the vertebrae of the neck during the lowering phase of the movement. Care must also be taken to see that the weight does not get too far behind the trainer as he may seriously damage the arms and shoulders in attempting to control it. Many experienced weight trainers consider this the basic exercise for the shoulders.

A variation of this exercise is to alternately lower the bar to the chest and to the shoulders behind the head, thus combining the two exercises into one. The press behind the neck develops the arm extensors and the shoulders: triceps, deltoids, trapezius, and associated muscle groups.

Rowing Motion

The lifter picks the weight up with the palms turned in, bends over at the waist, flattening the back as much as possible and keeping the knees slightly bent, and lets the arms hang down. The weight is then pulled up to the chest, the elbows are allowed to go out so that they are more or less in line with the shoulders, and then the weight is lowered again (fig. 3.14). An effective variation is to pick up the weight with the palms turned outward and bring it to the waist, keeping the elbows as close to the sides as possible. A second variation is to load one end of a barbell, place the other in a corner, straddle the bar, and perform rowing motions in this fashion. Bars are available commercially which are hinged at the floor end. This keeps the base of the apparatus from moving around and damaging the woodwork.

Fig. 3.14.   Rowing Motion to the Chest.

These exercises develop the arm flexors and the back muscles: biceps, radialis, brachioradialis, deltoids, rhomboids, latissimus dorsi, teres major, and associated muscle groups. The first variation has more effect on the latissimus dorsi than do the other two techniques.

Some instructors contend that this position should never be assumed because the long lever and the weight of the trunk, head, arms, and resistance place a great strain on the lower back muscles. While the writer has never heard of anyone being injured while performing rowing motions, the position might be hazardous for those with lower back problems. It is safer if the exercise is performed with the head resting on some sort of a support, which will remove any possibility of back strain.

Wrestler's Bridge

The exerciser starts in the supine position on the floor with knees bent. Rock up onto the crown of the head, lifting the buttocks and shoulders from the floor. Men not accustomed to this exercise will find it rather strenuous and are likely to incur a very sore neck if they go at it too vigorously at first. After a period of training without a weight, the exerciser may take a barbell at the chest, thrust it to arm's length as he rocks up on his head, and lower it again to the chest as he returns to the starting position (fig. 3.15). The exerciser should conclude by assuming the prone position, rolling up on to the crown of the head, and vigorously exercising the neck in this position. A foam rubber pad or some other sort of protection will be needed to keep the scalp from hurting during bridges.

Photographs by Gene O'Connell

Fig. 3.15.   Wrestler's Bridge.

It is difficult to introduce much in the way of variation in neck exercises unless one buys a head strap from which weights can be suspended or a helmet on which they can be loaded or has a training partner with whom he can perform "bulling" and the other exercises employed by wrestlers. One alternative to the towel exercises frequently used when a partner is available is to hang an inner tube from a hook, place the head inside, and flex the neck muscles in every possible direction against the elastic resistance provided by the tube. Another is a cable run from a head strap over a pulley mounted on the wall and then to a holder for weights.

The principal superficial muscle visibly affected by neck exercises is the sternocleidomastoid. Although a large number of associated muscle groups are also affected, they are difficult to differentiate in the living subject.

Many experienced exercisers would probably add one or more of the following movements to the foregoing program. It would be just as well not to include them at the beginning of training, but if desired they could be employed after one becomes somewhat accustomed to the exertion of barbell training.

Wrist Curls

The exerciser sits with forearms on thighs (fig. 3.16) or on a table. If preferred, kneel down and use the flat bench in place of a table. Hold a barbell in the hands, palms up. The wrists are alternately extended and flexed through the full range of movement. This exercise may also be performed with the palms down, in which case it is known as the **reverse wrist curl.**

The wrist curl develops the flexors of the forearm: flexor carpi radialis, flexor carpi ulnaris, and associated muscle groups. The reverse wrist curl develops the extensors of the forearm: extensor carpi radialis, extensor carpi ulnaris, and associated muscle groups.

An alternate exercise is the **wrist roller.** A cord is run through a hole drilled through the middle of a short piece of wood or pipe. Weights are suspended from the cord. The exerciser holds the bar in front of him with both hands and rotates it so that the cord wraps around the bar. Such a unit may be easily mounted on a wall if desired. In use, a set in which the bar is revolved in one direction is followed by a set in which it is rotated in the other.

Most people find that the forearms, like the calves, are very difficult to develop. To save possible disappointment, it should be pointed out that while the correlation between the girth of the forearm and the strength of the hand grip is moderately high, development of a strong grip requires movements specifically designed to exercise the finger and thumb flexors in addition to forearm training. These may include grasping a heavy barbell plate and passing it from one hand to the other, carrying a sack of sand or some similar material by one car, squeezing a sponge rubber ball, taking a sheet of newspaper by one corner and crumpling it up into a tight ball in one hand, or using any of the numerous spring resistance devices to be found on the market.

Shoulder Shrug

Stand in front of the barbell, squat, grasp the bar with the hands, and stand erect. Then contract the shrugging muscles, raise the shoulders as high as possible as though trying to touch the deltoids to the ears (fig. 3.17). Most persons seem to prefer to work with the palms turned out. The exercise may

Photographs by Gene Mozee

Fig. 3.16.   Wrist Curls.   Fig. 3.17.   Shoulder Shrug.

also be done with the weight held in front, in which case the palms are usually turned in. In either case the shoulder elevators are developed: trapezius, levator scapulae, rhomboid, and associated muscle groups.

Triceps Extension (French Press; Triceps Press)

The exerciser stands or sits with the barbell overhead at arm's length as though completing a press. The arms must be close to the ears. The upper arms are kept in this position while the elbows are flexed so that the bar comes down in back of the head. The elbows must be kept perpendicular while the bar is being raised (fig. 3.18). The exerciser will find that there is a decided tendency for them to move outward if the weight is a little on the heavy side. While this is an excellent exercise, it has the reputation of producing sore elbows and some individuals may find it impossible to use it.

A variation of this exercise can be done by lying supine on a bench, pressing the weight to arm's length, and then lowering and raising it as described.

Additional Exercises

Individuals with a large abdomen may wish to add bent knee sit-ups, leg raises, and vee-ups to this program in order to directly exercise their abdominal muscles. The difficulty of the first two movements may be increased by use of an inclined board.

Photographs by Gene Mozee

Fig. 3.18.   Triceps Extension.

WEIGHTS AND REPETITIONS

As was explained in Chapter 1, the results of a program of progressive resistance exercise seem to depend upon three variables: (1) the amount of stress placed on the muscles, (2) the duration of the exercise periods, and (3) the frequency of the exercise periods. The possible combinations of these three factors and the range of human differences in response to each are so great that researchers have hardly scratched the surface of their possible combinations. We do not even know whether programs designed to produce hypertrophy should differ from those designed to produce strength and, if so, in what ways. As a result of these factors the following suggestions are empirical rather than scientific.

The novice should start with weights which can be handled with comparative ease. As a rough guide for the person not accustomed to hard work the following is offered: press—one-fourth of body weight, curl—ten pounds less than the press, bench press—ten pounds more than the press, back and leg exercises—one-half of the body weight. It will usually be observed that after the first two or three weeks the beginner suddenly finds himself able to handle considerably more weight, especially in such exercises as the bench press. This does not mean that strength has greatly increased in that short period. It results from the fact that the exerciser has learned how to balance the weight, how to relax antagonistic muscles, and otherwise how to improve coordination. At that time the amounts of weight employed in the various exercises will need to be adjusted upward. Thereafter the exerciser should be able to remain on a schedule for changes in weights and repetitions.

The general rule is that a man begins with five or six repetitions of each exercise for the arms and ten or twelve for the back and legs. He works out three days a week: Monday, Wednesday, and Friday. (The idea of a rest every other day appears to have been one of Alan Calvert's contributions to weight training.) It should be anticipated that with proper warm-up, rest pauses, and the like, the exercise period will approximate two hours. Each Monday he adds one repetition to the arm exercises and two to the back and leg exercises. After a week of ten or twelve repetitions for the arms and twenty or twenty-four for the back and legs, he increases the weights for the former by five pounds and for the latter by ten pounds, and returns to the original five/six and ten/twelve repetitions. There is, of course, an end point to any progression. Sooner or later there will come a time at which the increment must be smaller than suggested. Eventually they may be measured in ounces.

The foregoing method is known as the **double progressive system,** since both the weights and the number of repetitions are increased at regular intervals. The older **single progressive system** consisted of keeping the repetitions at a given number but adding weight as frequently as possible. It is seldom seen today except among competitive lifters. Less popular now than some years ago is the "1001 Exercises" system. This assumes that the best way to develop muscles is to exercise them in a large number of different ways so that every fiber is stressed. The training program may be changed almost weekly in order to gain new approaches. For some reason this does not seem to work out as well as one would expect. Quite possibly the number of exercises included in such a program necessitates a reduction in the intensity of the effort put into each one. Generally speaking, greater development seems to result from more concentrated methods, but this system may have some advantages for those seeking extreme definition of muscle.

PROGRAM EVALUATION

To a large extent any program, basic or advanced, can be evaluated by the question. How do you feel the next morning? If you are unable to sleep, wake up exhausted, and have to drag yourself out of bed and through the day, you are probably overtraining. All too often the beginner finds his measurements shrinking and his strength decreasing. In desperation he drives himself to still greater exertion. This is precisely the wrong thing to do. A Mr. America may have to train every day if he is to keep in top competitive condition, but it is during the rest periods that his muscles build up. Proper rest is just as important as is proper exercise. The forty-year-old man may find that two workouts a week suit him best. Some experienced trainers recommend that every six weeks of hard training be followed by one week away from the weights. When training is resumed, the exercise program is changed. If nothing else, this breaks up the monotony, and a man goes back to his workouts rested and with renewed enthusiasm.

Advanced
training methods

4

One factor which stands out in all studies of progressive resistance exercise is the great individual differences in response to training programs. This makes it impossible to specify a standard program which will be equally suitable for everyone. The exercises, weights, and repetitions suggested in the previous chapter are just that—suggestions. The conclusion would seem to be that any schedule is more or less experimental and must be carefully observed to determine whether it is producing the desired results. Even when the results are satisfactory it must be anticipated that sooner or later an exerciser will reach a point at which he decides that he is no longer progressing as fast as he should. This is an indication that the time has come to switch to advanced training methods. Two different approaches are possible: changes in the system of training and in the use of apparatus. These will be discussed in that order. The reader may wonder why, if there are superior systems, he should not start with them instead of wasting time on a basic program. All advanced training methods depend upon one basic principle: increasing the amount of stress placed upon the body within the given training period. The beginning weight trainer is no more ready for these levels of work than is a college wrestler prepared for competition on the first day of team workouts. Only rarely should one consider advanced training methods until completion of six months or more on the basic program. Even longer may be advisable. Joe Abbenda, who has held the Mr. America and both the amateur and professional Mr. Universe titles, has stated that he spent the first two years of his training performing just three exercises: the squat, the dead lift, and the bench press.

SYSTEMS OF TRAINING

In Chapter 3 we presented the single progressive and double progressive systems. There are a number of others, the most popular of which are presented below. It must be said, however, that there is an increasing amount of research evidence which indicates that there is no significant difference in the end results provided the body is pushed to the same level of effort under each system.

Light and Heavy System

The trainer starts out with a weight considerably lighter than maximal, does a few (perhaps three) repetitions, stops, adds more weight (perhaps five pounds), and performs a few more repetitions, continuing this procedure as long as possible. Toward the end of such a series the amount of weight added may be decreased to the point that it consists of no more than a couple of iron washers, and the number of repetitions may be decreased from three to two, and finally to one. This was the method followed by the Egyptians during the years that they were the world's best weight lifters and is still advocated today by many men whose main interest is in the development of strength.

Heavy and Light System

This procedure has been popularized by the lifters at York, Pennsylvania. The individual starts off with the maximum weight which can be handled for a given number of repetitions, completes these, takes off some weight, and again repeats a maximal number of repetitions, repeating this procedure as long as can be continued. The basic principle is to keep the muscle working against near-maximal resistance even though fatigue is reducing its capacity for performance. There is some evidence that this method of training is more effective than is the light and heavy system. This technique is very popular in rehabilitation work where it is often referred to as the Zinovieff or the Oxford technique.

A variation of this program is to have fellow trainers remove approximately 20 per cent of the weight as soon as the exerciser falters, so that the exercise continues without interruption. This is known as the **multipoundage system**. It was introduced by Henry J. Atkin in England about 1949 and is more popular there than in the United States. One difficulty with it is that it requires a fairly large assortment of weights in order to make the changes, and at least three men must work out together.

Step Bombing

Advanced exercisers sometimes combine the two foregoing systems by starting with a weight with which they can do say ten repetitions. After each rest period five pounds is added. When they can perform only a single repetition, five pounds is removed between sets until they are back to the starting weight.

Blitz Program

The exerciser trains five days a week, but works on only one group of muscles on each day. For instance, Monday might be devoted to the arm flexors, Tuesday to the arm extensors, Wednesday to back and chest exercises, Thursday to the legs, and Friday to the abdomen. Bruce Page recommends that each exercise be performed for five sets of six repetitions each. The goal is to keep a limited muscle area flushed with blood for a prolonged period. Like the every-hour-on-the-hour system, this is a very vigorous program and is usually followed for a comparatively short time. In effect it is a split routine carried to an extreme. Usually comparatively light weights are employed.

Cheating Exercises

These exercises were introduced to American weight trainers following Berry's observations of the training methods of the German Olympic Weight-Lifting Team at Los Angeles in 1932. They consist of using more weight than can be handled in strict form and then employing movements of other parts of the body (what kinesiologists term **synergistic muscle action**) to get the weight past the sticking point. In the two-hands curl, for instance, the problem is usually to get the weight started. Performed as a cheating exercise, the lifter leans forward at the waist and starts the lift by swinging the upper body backward. In the press first the hips are swung backward and then the weight is started upward by swinging them forward. The essential point is that the movement is performed in proper style once the sticking point is surmounted.

This form of exercise has much to recommend it as it enables the lifter to provide maximal resistance to the muscle through that portion of the range of motion in which it is strongest, whereas otherwise the resistance afforded is actually controlled by the amount it can handle through the range wherein it is weakest. Further, it simultaneously exercises other parts of the body which would be involved to only a relatively small degree if the strict style were followed. The value of the exercise is lost if the synergistic movements are performed in such a way as to merely throw the weight through the movement. Properly performed, this is an extremely effective system.

Circuit Training

Strength and endurance may be improved by a program which places the emphasis on a reduction of the time required to complete a given exercise program. A circuit consists of a number of stations, at each of which one exercise is performed. The loads should be about one-half of one's maximal effort. A trial is given to see how long it takes to complete this series of exercises and then a target time is assigned approximately one-third faster than the recorded time. As soon as the person can complete the circuit in this time, the loads are increased; the exercise is timed again, and a new target time is established. Variations are possible in the number of exercises and the number of times one goes around the circuit. The circuit may be **biased** to give specialized or increased amounts of work to certain muscles or areas of the body.

This form of training is popular with athletes and the armed forces of the world (fig. 4.1) as it provides the cardiorespiratory stress which is lacking in most systems designed to develop strength.

Compound Exercises

Exercises pressed for time may combine two exercises into one. For instance, do a curl or a reverse curl and continue the movement on into a press, or a press while executing a squat, or a deep knee bend followed by a heel raise, or a bent arm pull-over followed by a press. This may have been the ancestor of the superset system, but possesses the disadvantage that the weight used will be governed by the amount which can be handled in the movement in which the person is weaker.

Peripheral Heart Action (PHA or Sequence) System

This is the opposite of the blitz program. The emphasis here is on keeping the blood in constant circulation through the muscular system so that it will bring a steady supply of oxygen, nourishment, and buffers to a given area and remove metabolic wastes and prevent congestion. This is done by arranging groups of five or six exercises, called a **sequence**, in such a way that each exercise affects a different part of the body. For example, a sequence might consist of the press, rowing motion, sit-up, heel raise, and dead lift. Each exercise is performed for eight to ten repetitions, and each sequence is repeated two to five times. The exerciser then goes on to another sequence, performing in all a total of four to six sequences. No rest is taken between exercises or sequences; the exerciser goes right through one and into the next. Proponents of this system claim that they can take a heavier workout with less fatigue and quicker recovery, but generally concede that it is better adapted for producing strength and definition than muscular size.

Rest-Pause System

The weight trainer does a single movement, using close to his maximal weight, rests a minute or two, does a second movement, rests, and repeats this process until the muscle is fatigued. This seems better fitted for the production of strength than hypertrophy.

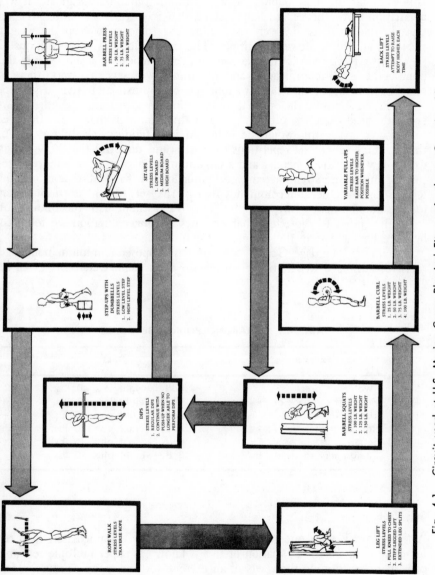

Fig. 4.1.   Circuit used at U.S. Marine Corps Physical Fitness Academy, Quantico, Virginia.

Set System

The use of sets seems to have been introduced by Hise in the 1940s and is now by far the most popular advanced training method. Originally it was a variation of the heavy and light system, that is, in each set lighter weights than in the previous one were used. Now the trend is to keep the weight the same and to use fewer repetitions. The trainer does several repetitions of an exercise, rests, repeats the exercise, rests, and repeats it again. While the number of repetitions in a set and the number of sets may vary, there is some good evidence that three to four sets of approximately five to six repetitions each comprise the optimal combination for increasing strength.[1] However, advanced exercisers often use two or three times as many sets. In order to conserve space, this would be indicated in a training schedule as 3 x 6, that is, three sets of six repetitions each. It seems doubtful that heavy loads with a few repetitions per set and a large number of sets are any more effective for improving strength than are lighter loads with more repetitions and fewer sets. MacQueen[2] recommends four or five sets of ten repetitions each for the development of hypertrophy. This is consistent with the findings of scientific studies to the effect that exercises of longer duration are followed by a greater increase in the volume of the muscle.

    Training Poundage Goals. Steiner[3] has proposed minimum poundage goals for advanced weight trainers using the set system. Details are given in Table 4.1.

TABLE 4.1.   TRAINING POUNDAGE GOALS

Exercise	Goal
Two-hands press	Body weight less 40 lbs.
Press off the back of the neck	Body weight less 50 lbs.
Bench press	Body weight plus 20 lbs.
Rowing motion	Body weight plus 20 lbs.
Squat	Body weight plus 75 lbs.
Straight-legged dead lift	Body weight plus 50 lbs.

Supersets

A set of exercises for one group of muscles is followed immediately by a set for their antagonists. A variation of this is known as **super multiple sets** and consists of performing three sets of an exercise for one group of muscles followed by the same number of sets for their antagonists. A short rest is taken between sets. In the considered opinion of Peary Rader, this is the most effective system for building the arms. These are extremely fatiguing methods and are recommended only for experienced men.

Split Routines

Individuals pressed for time or on a very heavy training program may pursue a split routine. This means that on one day they exercise only the upper body and the next day only the lower body. It is, of course, necessary to work out six days a week. Opinion is divided as to the desirability of this method. Some feel that it has no advantages over a normal program; others contend that a split program enables them to accomplish more exercise than they would otherwise without inducing overfatigue.

Burns

Some weight trainers follow their initial repetitions with a series of rapid half-contractions. This produces a burning sensation in the muscle—hence the name. They believe that this forces an additional amount of blood into the muscle and causes a greater increase in size. The writer knows of no research study in which this theory has been evaluated.

Summary

There is little in the way of research material to indicate the comparative values of these programs and their numerous variations. Men like John Grimek developed some of the great physiques of our time before blitz programs and other such methods were introduced. If the contemporary programs do nothing else, however, they introduce some welcome variety into training schedules which might otherwise become boring. Perhaps they serve to retain the interest of weight trainers who would otherwise fall by the wayside. Certainly they provide a fertile field of study for those interested in the scientific side of exercise.

Even with the best of systems the average person may anticipate that the forearms and calves will prove difficult to develop, so do not become discouraged if they fail to respond as promptly as you would like. What has worked for someone else may or may not work for you. If you are not getting the results you think you should be, do not hesitate to experiment with other exercises, but give your new program sufficient time—say three months—to show its merits before abandoning it.

USE OF APPARATUS

During the last few years the weight trainers have developed a great deal of apparatus to help them attain maximal strength and hypertrophy. Some of it is ingenious, but complicated. Fortunately some of the most effective is also the most simple and can be built by almost anyone. There is available from *Iron Man Magazine* a helpful pamphlet entitled *Twenty Simplified Plans of Weight Training Equipment*[4] which provides dimensions, bills for materials, and the like. The apparatus described can easily be constructed by any "hammer mechanic."

Incline Bench (Slant Board)

One of the simplest and most common pieces of apparatus seen in weight-training gymnasia is the incline bench (fig. 4.2). This was originally designed so that the angle of the incline could be changed. The idea was that if it were slowly increased the trainer would eventually be able to press in the standing position the same amount which was originally used in the bench press. This method of training seems to be largely forgotten. Most boards are now either built on a 45-degree slant or put in that position and left there so that the exerciser is in effect working in a position midway between supine and standing. It is especially valuable for pressing and flying motions, although curls and numerous other exercises can be performed on it with profit.

When a strap is fixed across the top so that the exerciser can insert the feet under it and place the head at the bottom, it is referred to as a decline board. Most people find a 45-degree incline too extreme and prefer to use one with a lesser gradient. Pressing done in this position is especially popular as it imparts a different stress to the pectorals and contributes to their full development.

Hopper

The hopper was originated by Hise. It is seldom seen in the gymnasium today, but in the writer's opinion is an extremely valuable aid. The construction is diagrammed in figure 4.3 and can be built quite easily. In use the exerciser stands in the center, lifts the barbell, and lets it come down hard so that the weight rebounds slightly. The hopper raises the bar high enough so that the period during which the upper body "hangs from its ligaments" during dead

Photograph courtesy of Iron Man Industries

Fig. 4.2. Adjustable Incline Bench.

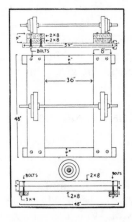

Fig. 4.3. Diagram for Construction of a Hopper.

lifting is eliminated. This protects the lifter from back injuries. At the same time the amount of weight which can be handled is considerably increased. It will be noted that use of this apparatus introduces the principle of "elastic rebound" into dead lifting.

The disadvantages of this piece of apparatus are the thunderous noise and the shock which results when a heavy weight is banged down on it. It certainly has no place in an upstairs room if one has any regard for the plaster on the ceiling below. A rather ingenious solution to this problem was used by some of the earlier competitive dead lifters. These men dug a hole in the ground and stood in it while lifting the barbell. This enabled them to use a weight too heavy to be handled in the normal manner. As their strength increased, they began to fill in the hole, eventually arriving back at floor level. The basic idea, of course, is similar to the use of the adjustable incline board as a connecting link between the flat bench and the standing press. It would seem that the same thing could be more easily accomplished by lifting the weight from blocks and gradually decreasing their height.

Lat Machine

Probably the most popular piece of apparatus in the average gymnasium is the latissimus dorsi machine because of its demonstrated value in developing those muscles and thus producing the **V**-shape so admired by body builders. Normally the man kneels or sits in front of it and pulls the bar down to his shoulders behind his head, although it is sometimes pulled down in front of the head as shown in fig. 4.4. There are differently shaped bars, and they are said to have different effects on the muscles. Another popular exercise is to keep the elbows extended and swing the bar down in front of the body as though the arms were pivoted at the shoulders. A triceps extension movement is also popular. The bar is grasped with the forearms parallel to the floor. The elbows are then fully extended, with every effort being made to prevent any movement of the upper arms or body. This is usually called the triceps pull down.

As his strength increases, a light man may find the weight tends to lift him up, and he may require a fixed seat with a belt attached to hold him in place.

A rather unusual exercise employing this piece of apparatus is curls performed while lying supine on the floor.

Leg Press Machine

One of the most popular pieces of gymnasium equipment is the leg press machine (fig. 4.5). While it cannot be seen in figure 4.5, there is a small triangular platform which fits under and raises the hips, thereby flattening the lower back and reducing the chance of injury. It develops much the same muscles as does the squat, but a great deal more weight can be handled with this apparatus than in the squat as it is not necessary to lift the body in addition to the weight. However, research indicates that there is no significant difference between the strength gains resulting from the use of this apparatus and those resulting from the practice of squats.[5]

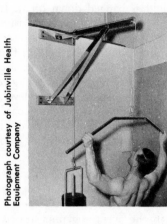

Fig. 4.4.   Lat Machine.

Fig. 4.5.   Leg Press Machine.

A popular exercise for the calves performed with this machine is shown in figure 4.6. The exercise is known as the **donkey raise** and is illustrated so clearly that no explanation is required. The exercise can also be performed in the inverted position.

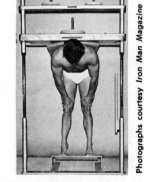

Fig. 4.6.   Donkey Raises.

Knee Flexion and Extension Machine

The uses of this machine are so well shown in figure 4.7 that there is no necessity for a description. Its great virtue is that it furnishes resistance throughout the range of movement. If prone knee flexion is performed with an iron boot, gravity takes over once the weight passes the perpendicular, and it then becomes a matter of contracting the extensors to keep it from falling on the exerciser. There is no other piece of apparatus known to the writer which quite replaces this item.

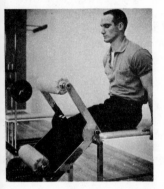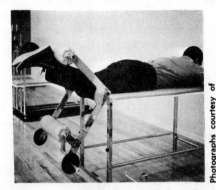

Photographs courtesy of Paramount Gymnasium Equipment Corp.

Fig. 4.7.   Knee Flexion and Extension Machine.

Calf Machine

The calf machine comes in a large range of designs, but all are essentially ways of conveniently resting the resistance on the shoulders while doing heel raises. The example shown in figure 4.8 is one of the simpler models; some are engineered to work through a lever system. In any case they are excellent devices for working these hard-to-develop muscles through their full range of movement.

Photograph courtesy of Strength & Health

Fig. 4.8.   Jack Delinger, Mr. America 1949 and Mr. Universe 1956, Exercising on a Calf Machine.

Variable Resistance Machines

An example of a popular variable resistance machine is seen in figure 4.9. As has been explained earlier (see p. 3), this apparatus is designed to afford a relatively constant degree of resistance throughout the entire range of motion of a joint. When using a barbell the exerciser is limited to the amount of weight that can be moved through the point of the poorest mechanical advantage. At all other points the muscles are exercised at suboptimal levels. The variable resistance feature automatically compensates for changes in mechanical advantage and maintains a relatively stable load-to-strength ratio.

Almost any standard weight-training exercise can be practiced on these machines, and a number of men can work out at one time. The fact that the weights are under constant control is an important safety factor.

Isometric Rack

The isometric rack is sometimes called the **power rack.** This name is highly inappropriate. Technically, power is equal to the work accomplished divided by the time required to do it. In isometric exercise the bar is not moved, and

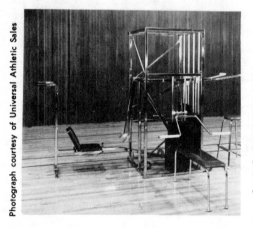

Photograph courtesy of Universal Athletic Sales

Fig. 4.9. A Popular Type of Variable Resistance Apparatus. The cantilevers to which the weights are attached are designed to afford optimal resistance at point in the range of motion of a joint as alterations occur in the mechanical efficiency of the levers and the muscles which operate them.

no work is accomplished. While some use is made of isometric exercise as an adjunct to weight training, it is difficult to determine the extent to which it is actually employed. When it is utilized, the most common procedure seems to be to determine the sticking point in a given exercise. A bar is then fixed at this level, and the man exercises against it isometrically in hope of developing his strength to the extent that he can move an actual weight through this point (fig. 4.10). The writer knows of no research in which this method of training has been evaluated, and claims for its benefits must be treated with caution. This piece of apparatus may also be used to confine a barbell to a given range of movement, thus reducing the possibility of injury.

Photograph courtesy of John Grimek

Fig. 4.10. Tommy Kono, who has held World Weight Lifting Championships at two different weights, practicing isometric exercise at the sticking point in the two-hands press.

Those who desire to experiment with the isometric rack as an aid in sports training might be interested in using a system such as the one devised by Bruno[6] for football players. The exercises consist of the squat, dead lift, bench press, and upright rowing motion. On Monday they are performed with the bar at a low level, on Wednesday with the bar at an intermediate level, and on Friday with the bar at a high level. Two sets of three-to-five repetitions are performed. The great drawback to this form of training is that it does nothing to improve cardiorespiratory condition.

REFERENCES

1. R. T. Withers. "Effect of Varied Weight Training Loads on the Strength of University Freshmen," *Research Quarterly*, 41:110-114, March, 1970.
2. I. J. MacQueen. "Recent Advances in the Technique of Progressive Resistance Exercise," *British Medical Journal*, 2:1193-1198, November 20, 1954.
3. Bradley J. Steiner. "Choosing Your Correct Poundages," *Iron Man*, 33:22 *et seq.*, January, 1974.
4. Stephen Kazan. "20 Simplified Plans of Weight Training Equipment." Alliance, Nebraska: *Iron Man* Magazine.
5. Larry A. Burleson. "Two Types of Weight Training Exercise and Their Relationship to Leg Strength Development Among Selected Male Students at Chico State College, 1968." Unpublished Graduate Study, Chico State College, 1969.
6. Frederick W. Bruno. "Power Rack Training for Football," *Athletic Journal*, 53:*et seq.*, September 1972.

The use
of dumbbells

5

Nearly any exercise that can be done with a barbell can be duplicated with dumbbells. The latter, however, frequently have special advantages of their own. Often they create more stress on the muscles than do the barbells. In the press, for instance, the even distribution of the weight on a barbell tends to inhibit any tendency for the bar to move sideways, whereas dumbbells require a powerful contraction of the shoulder muscles to keep them from dropping to the sides. Few individuals can press as much with two dumbbells as they can with one barbell. In the curl the bar inhibits the tendency of the biceps to turn the forearms into a supine position. Most men, nevertheless, prefer barbells to dumbbells. Among the older weight trainers the latter have a reputation for making a person stiff. The reason for this was never clear to the writer, and he has not personally experienced this effect. Unfortunately, researchers have ignored the study of dumbbell training, and we have no real information on its value as compared with barbell exercises.

In the routine exercises such as the press and the curl most trainers seem to prefer "alternate" exercises, that is, one arm goes up as the other is coming down. Usually more weight can be handled in this way than when both are pressed or curled together, and it is easier to concentrate on the movement being made. There is, however, a decided tendency to use body movements to aid the arms. To avoid this many prefer to do such exercises either sitting or on the incline bench. While the writer has no scientific evidence to back up his opinion, he has a strong impression that a number of body builders famed for the girth of their arms spend an inordinate amount of time working with dumbbells either seated or on the incline bench.

While barbell exercises can be done with dumbbells, it does not follow that the reverse is true. There are a number of dumbbell exercises which cannot be performed with a barbell. Some of the more popular are described here.

Front Raise

Stand erect, with the dumbbells resting against the front of the thighs, elbows extended, palms in; raise them to shoulder height directly in front, swing the arms back until they are parallel to the shoulders, and then lower them to the sides. Next lift them back to shoulder height, swing them to the forward position, and lower them to the original starting position (fig. 5.1). The elbows must be kept extended throughout the exercise.

Fig. 5.1.   Front Raise.

A variation is to start the movements by raising the arms until the dumbbells are overhead and then lowering them to shoulder height. Another variation is to lean forward at the waist, the arms hanging down, and then raise the dumbbells as high as possible while keeping them in line with the shoulders (fig. 5.2). This is known as the **bent over lateral raise.** These exercises develop the shoulders and upper back: deltoids, supraspinatus, upper trapezius, and associated muscle groups.

A **side raise,** done while lying on one side on a bench, is also popular.

Dumbbell Swing

The exerciser bends over with the elbows extended and the dumbbell held between the legs with both hands, knees semiflexed. The dumbbell is swung upward, keeping the elbows extended. The feet do not move, but the exerciser comes to a semierect position (fig. 5.3). One variation is to swing the dumbbell in one hand, with the free hand placed on the knee. The hands may be changed at the top of the swing so that the swing is made with each hand alternately. Another is to swing the dumbbell up and to squat or to take a lunging step forward at the same time. A dumbbell may be used in each hand, starting them outside of the legs and swinging them both at once.

While these variations affect the body in somewhat different ways, the general purpose is to develop the muscles of the lower back: the spinae erectors and associated muscle groups. The shoulders, especially the deltoids, also benefit. Dumbbell swings must not be done until the exerciser is well warmed up, or back strain may be suffered.

Fig. 5.2. Bent Over Lateral Raise.

Photographs by Gene Mozee

Fig. 5.3. Dumbbell Swing.

Flying Motion

The exerciser is supine on a flat bench, arms extended in line with the shoulders but partially flexed at the elbows. The arms are crossed over the chest and then returned to the starting position. The arms are alternated each time they are crossed so that one is uppermost one time and the other the next (fig. 5.4).

A variation of this is to do the exercise with the elbows straight. This is known as the **supine** or **straight-arm lateral raise** and is open to the same

Photographs by Gene O'Connell

Fig. 5.4. Flying Motion.

objection as is the straight-arm pull-over. Either form, however, develops the shoulders and upper chest and back: deltoids, pectoralis major, middle trapezius, and associated muscle groups.

Hise Deltoid Exercise

The exerciser grasps a doorway or some other brace with one hand. The arm is extended, but with most individuals there is a slight bend in the elbow, and the torso is usually at a slight angle backward. The exercise starts with the weight overhead, elbow extended and upper arm close to the head, as though a press had just been completed. The dumbbell is lowered rapidly to the shoulder and at once rebounded to arm's length. The supporting arm prevents body movement which might aid in the exercise and relieves the exerciser from any worries about retaining balance. The collars must be set up tightly as the rapid rebounding will tend to loosen them. As the name indicates, this exercise is designed primarily to influence the deltoids, but the triceps and upper shoulder muscle groups in general benefit from it. It will be noted that this is another example of "elastic rebound" training. While exercise physiologists have recently become interested in this form of activity, the writer has yet to see a paper on the subject which acknowledges Hise's pioneering work in the field.

One-Arm Push

The man stands erect with the dumbbell at the shoulder and the opposite foot a little advanced. As the weight is pushed up, the hand turns so that the palm is rotated forward, almost on a line with the shoulders, the knees are flexed a little, the torso bends forward and is supported by the free forearm coming to rest on the knee of the advanced leg. The hip on the lifting side must be thrust backward as a counterbalance. Most lifters find it easier to control the weight if they look upward at it. Many prefer to put their free hand on the advanced knee as they begin to lean forward and then slide the forearm across it. In this way they are never left unsupported. The weight is kept a little back of the center line of the body.

This exercise is excellent for practically all of the muscles of the shoulder and back as well as for the arm extensors. In an advanced form this movement develops into the **bent press**. This is now an almost forgotten lift, but when it was in its heyday a good bent presser could put up as much weight with one arm in this style as he could press with both arms in the usual manner.

Side Bend

The exerciser stands erect, the dumbbell at the side, bends as far to that side as possible, and then returns to the erect position (fig. 5.5). This movement exercises the lateral flexors: abdominis oblique, erector spinae, and associated muscle groups.

Wrist Abduction

The dumbbell is loaded at one end. The exerciser stands erect, arms at the sides or with the free arm on the hip, and grasps the weight by the free end. Drop the wrist as far as possible and then cock it up as high as possible (fig. 5.6). This exercises the forearm abductors: flexor carpi radialis, extensor carpi radialis, and associated muscle groups.

Photographs by Gene O'Connell

Fig. 5.5. Side Bend.   Fig. 5.6. Wrist Abduction.

Wrist Adduction

The dumbbell is loaded as before but grasped so that the weight is to the back instead of forward. The movement is made through the full range of movement. This exercises the forearm adductors: flexor carpi ulnaris, extensor carpi ulnaris, and associated muscle groups.

A friend wants to participate in a wrist wrestling tournament. His only piece of apparatus is a dumbbell. Which single exercise would you suggest he practice? Why?

Forearm Supination-Pronation

The exerciser sits with one forearm on his knee as for wrist curls, the hand holding a dumbbell. The forearm is rotated from full supination to full pronation. This works the forearm supinators and pronators: biceps, supinator, pronator quadratus, and associated muscle groups. A variation is to grip the free end of a dumbbell loaded at the other and to supinate and pronate the forearm.

Zottman Curl

The exerciser either stands erect or bends over at the waist, with a dumbbell held between the legs and the free hand on the knee. Curl the weight, pronate the forearm, and lower the weight to the starting point. It is then reverse curled to the chest, the forearm is supinated, and the weight is lowered again (fig. 5.7). The amount of weight that can be handled in this exercise

Fig. 5.7.   Steps in the Zottman Curl.

will, of course, be controlled by the degree of strength which can be exerted in the reverse curl. This is an excellent exercise for the elbow flexors and the forearm supinators and pronators: biceps, brachialis, brachioradialis, supinator, pronator quadratus, and associated muscle groups.

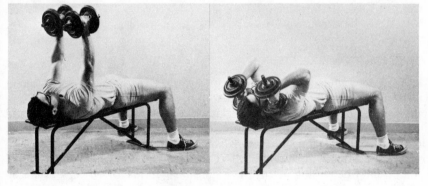

Fig. 5.8.   Triceps Extension on Bench with Dumbbells.

Triceps Extension on Bench with Dumbbells

This exercise will be recognized as a variation on the standard method of using a barbell in the standing position as described in Chapter 3. The man lies on his back on a bench, both arms fully extended upward, as though completing a supine press with dumbbells. While the upper arms are kept elevated, the elbows are flexed and then extended (fig. 5.8). Like the barbell exercise, the effect is largely on the elbow extensors: the triceps.

Dumbbell High Pull-Up

The exerciser assumes a lunge position, with the dumbbell close to the forward foot. Pull it as nearly as possible straight up, ending in a position somewhat similar to that of a high pull-up (fig. 5.9). Care must be taken that the hand is not turned over and the weight pressed into the final position. This is an excellent exercise for the arm flexors and upper shoulder muscles: biceps, brachialis, brachioradialis, deltoids, supraspinatus, trapezius, and associated muscle groups.

Photographs by Gene Mozee

Fig. 5.9.   Steps in Dumbbell High Pull-Up.

CONCENTRATION EXERCISES

The basic idea underlying concentration exercises is to employ a movement which insofar as possible is restricted to the use of a given muscle group, to stabilize the joint so that accessory muscle movement is eliminated, and then to focus one's full concentration on the muscle group being exercised. How important the concentration factor is we do not know. Generally such exercises are done with a dumbbell as it is difficult to secure the required stabilization when using a barbell. Figure 5.10 shows the triceps extension exercise done as a concentration exercise. The reader will observe that the free hand is used to firmly anchor the weight-bearing arm alongside the ear, thus ensuring that the exercise is done without aid from accessory muscles

Fig. 5.10.   Concentration Triceps Extension Exercise.

or body movement. Having nothing to think of except relaxing and contracting the triceps, the exerciser is free to devote his undivided attention to this one muscle. Alternatively, this exercise may be done using both hands to hold the dumbbell, with the little fingers against one end of the dumbbell.

Concentration Curl

Perhaps the most common exercise of this type is the concentration curl. Sit with the elbow firmly braced against the leg, as shown in figure 5.11. It is kept in this position during the entire movement. A variation is to sit in a chair, keeping one's back in contact with the back of the chair throughout the entire movement. Another is to stand behind an incline board, with the upper arm and elbow resting on the board. The forearm is extended until the arm is straight. The elbow is then flexed again without permitting the upper

Fig. 5.11.   Concentration Curl.

arm and the elbow to lose contact with the board. This is known as the **preacher curl**. One respected gymnasium owner argues that usually these stands are too high. He recommends that the top of the stand be three inches lower than the bottom of the pectorals. The exercise can be practiced with the hands about three inches apart and the elbows about 20 inches apart, and also with the hands and elbows both about eleven inches apart.

Another technique is to lie prone on a bench with the arms hanging down over the edge of the bench and to do curls while the edge of the bench prevents any backward movement of the arms. This is frequently shown in magazine articles, but is attended by difficulties in performance. Unless the bench is comparatively high off the floor, it will not be possible to extend the elbows fully. The average bench is designed primarily for bench presses and is too narrow for this sort of curling. Finally, the edge of the bench cuts into the triceps and is extremely uncomfortable.

The Concentration Dumbbell Rowing Motion

This exercise is shown in figure 5.12. Actually, the body is not too well braced in this position, and some care is required to make sure that the movement is not assisted by rotation of the torso.

There are, of course, other concentration exercises, but all work on the same principle, that is, of isolating the action of a muscle or a muscle group to as complete an extent as is possible.

Photographs by Gene Mozee

Fig. 5.12.   Concentration Dumbbell Rowing Motion.

After practicing the concentration triceps extension, curl, and dumbbell rowing motion, what is your subjective opinion about the importance of the concentration factor? Can you suggest ways in which several other exercises could be adapted to include the concentration element?

SWING BELL

A swing bell is simply a dumbbell with the plates moved to the center so that the ends are left free for use as handles. As a result it must be used like a barbell rather than like a dumbbell. A typical swing bell exercise, the **front raise**, is shown in figure 5.13. In the writer's opinion these are awkward to use and have no particular advantages over dumbbells and barbells other than to introduce a bit of variety into the training program.

Fig. 5.13.   Front Raise with Swing Bell.

IRON BOOT

The iron boot is simply a device for attaching a dumbbell to the feet. The most common exercises performed with it are the following:

1. Standing—knee flexion, straight-leg raise in front, in back and to the side.
2. Sitting—knee extension. It should be mentioned that many therapists discourage use of this exercise as a means of restoring strength to an injured knee, as they believe the weight tends to pull the joint apart when the knee is at the 90° angle. They prefer to use a machine such as is shown in figure 4.9 or one in which a cable is attached to the shoe and runs under the seat to the weight holder, thus relieving the knee of the need for supporting the resistance.
3. Supine lying—leg raise with knee straight, leg spread, inverted bicycle ride
4. Prone lying—knee flexion
5. Side lying—leg raising

Weight
training for women

6

The President's Council on Physical Fitness and Sports has said that most American women lack the necessary strength in their arms, shoulders, and trunk to perform the ordinary tasks required in daily living. Lack of strength frequently imposes limitations on performance even in women athletes. While there is no question that weight training is the quickest way to develop strength, most women have been afraid that weight training would increase muscular bulk, giving them a masculine appearance. As late as 1960 Chew could write that there was "a lack of information on the use of weights for girls as this is an entirely new concept in the field of curriculum."[1] Apparently she could find only a single paper[2] on the subject. The picture has changed considerably since then. Perhaps the major innovation in the training of women athletes has been the increased emphasis on progressive resistance exercise. Coaches seem generally agreed that the sensational showing made by the East German girls in the Montreal Olympics may be attributed largely to the fact that they spent 25 per cent of their training time in using weights. Nevertheless, this form of training is still relatively new to American women and is yet controversial in some quarters. Consequently the statements made in this chapter will be documented in some detail.

The quality of female muscle, i.e., contractile properties and ability to exert force, is the same as in the male. It follows that the female has the same potential for strength development as does the male of comparable size. She does not, however, have the same capacity for developing body size and muscular bulk because the secretion of the male hormone testosterone is considerably higher in the normal man than in the normal woman. Consequently the average woman's strength is about two-thirds that of a man.

Another reason for the lower strength-weight ratio in women as compared with men of equal weight is their smaller percentage of muscle in relation to their considerably larger amount of adipose tissue. Young women average 27 per cent of their body weight as fat, compared with 12 per cent for men.[3] Probably much of this difference is due to the women's lesser activity. The only morphological characteristic common to all outstanding athletes, male and female alike, is the low ratio of body fat and the high percentage of lean body mass. Olga Korbut, for instance, is said to have only 1.5 per cent body fat when in strict training.

Alterations in body composition as the result of a high resistance weight training program are nearly identical for both men and women—that is, there is an increase in lean body weight and a decrease in total body fat, with relativly little change in total body weight. [4, 5] In a study of college women MacIntyre[6] found that exercising as little as one-half an hour three times a week for seven weeks resulted in a significant reduction in fat and increase in muscle. Other investigators have reported similar findings.

While weight training significantly improves the body composition, it does not appear to be an effective method of reducing body weight. Most studies agree with Price's[7] finding that several weeks of weight training will produce little change in body weight. There is a large body of evidence to show that the difference between girls of normal weight and those of overweight is largely a matter of activity rather than of diet. In one study normalweight high school girls were shown to have an average intake of 2,706 calories daily, while their obese school mates averaged only 1,965 calories. While diet must be controlled, the daily difference in calorie use between an active and a sedentary woman can easily amount to 500 calories, which would consume a pound of fat in a week. Perhaps the most effective approach is to include running in the training program. However, some women have unusually low basal metabolic rates and find it extremely difficult to lose weight even on a regimen of this kind. This is particularly true of those who have been dieting for an extended period.

Mechanical Aids

Women patronizing commercial gymnasia seem to have a special fondness for belt vibrators, rollers, and other effortless "spot reducers." The claims of the hucksters notwithstanding, the bulk of the evidence indicates that these machines have no value for that purpose. There is no such thing as spot reducing which can result from massage or vibrating machines of any type. Research has shown that the fat content present in animal tissue is unchanged even when given massage forceful enough to produce multiple hemorrhages.[8] Mechanical vibrators are equally useless for this purpose.[9] Physiologists know of no mechanism of fat mobilization which supports the concept that they would be helpful.

Take an informal survey of your friends (male and female) to discover their beliefs about spot reducing and the use of vibrators and rollers. What could you say to clear up any misconceptions?

Exercise Programs

There is no need to devise special exercise schedules for females. The same programs are equally effective for both men and women. Wilmore,[4] for instance, successfully trained a coeducational class of college students on a program consisting of half squats or leg presses, toe raises, two hand curls, standing presses, bench presses, bent arm pullovers, bent rowing motions, and side bends. Price,[7] using women subjects only, employed a routine consisting of triceps extension, parallel squats, supine bench press, bent knee dead lift, two hands curl, side bend, latissimus pulldowns, and abdominal curls. The late George Bruce, who produced a large number of beauty contest winners, was probably the first to introduce strenuous weight training into their developmental programs. Amedee Chabot, twice Miss USA, was placed on the following program:

Warm up with dumbbells, 2 x 8
Sit ups, 3 x 15
Dumbbell swing, 3 x 10
Toe touches, 3 x 8
Dead lift, 3 x 8
Bench press, 3 x 8
Leg press, 3 x 8
Dumbbell squat, 3 x 8
Dumbbell lunge, 3 x 8

Any specific program and the poundages and repetitions used must, of course, be designed to suit the needs of the individual. Some suggestions for improving the most common figure faults are given in Table 6.1.

TABLE 6.1.   MOST COMMON FEMININE FIGURE FAULTS AND APPROPRIATE EXERCISES

Fault	Exercise
Conspicuous collar bones and/or undersized bust	Bent arm pull-overs; flying exercise; bench press with dumbbells
Large abdomen	Bent knee sit-ups; vee-ups; all forms of side bends and twists
Flabby thighs	Squats; leg press; front, side, and back leg raises; lunges and stair climbing with barbell on shoulders; leg flexion and extension with iron boot
Underdeveloped calves	Heel raises; walking on the toes with barbell on shoulders

Women athletes will, of course, have the advantage of being guided by their coaches. Their programs will often be quite strenuous. For example, Joan Lind (fig. 6.1), an Olympic silver medal winner in the single sculls, employs the following off-season training routine:

Fig. 6.1.   Joan Lind, a Magna Cum Laude graduate of California State University, Long Beach and America's premier oarswoman. Since the most severe stress in athletics is found in rowing, Ms. Lind surely presents the relatively low ratio of body fat and the high percentage of lean body mass characteristic of athletes. It is evident that this in no way detracts from the femininity of her appearance. (Photo by Anna Rivera, courtesy Dr. A. K. Thomas.)

Slant board leg raises, 2 x 25
Latissimus machine rowing, 4 x 10 with 110-150 lbs., depending on how much the back is used
Bench press, 3 x 10, 100-110 lbs.
Upright rowing, 4 x 10, 70 lbs.
Leg curls, 3 x 10, 50-60 lbs.
Leg extensions, 3 x 10, 100-110 lbs.
Leg presses, 4 x 10 with 290, 335, 360, and 385 lbs.
Chins, 3 x 5
Bent knee abdominal curls, 4 x 50
Parallel bar dips, 2 x 5.

Various studies have shown that women suffer more frequent dislocations of the patella and more joint sprains than do men. In part, at least, this may be due to their weaker musculature. Weight training appears to be the most rational approach to the prevention of such injuries. It should be known that the use of anabolic steroids for the purpose of stimulating muscular development is potentially as dangerous for women as it is for men. The American College of Sports Medicine's position paper on this subject lists masculinization, disruption of the normal growth pattern, voice changes, acne, hirsutism, enlargement of the clitoris, disturbances of the menstrual cycle, and possible upset of the reproduction function as among the undesired side effects of their use. The College urges that anyone involved in the care of female athletes "should exercise all persuasions available to prevent the use of anabolic steroids by female athletes."[10] It would be hard to put the case more strongly. Use of an iron supplement, however, may prove helpful in improving performance. This is a matter to be discussed with one's physician.

Figure Contouring

Quantifying goals to be pursued in figure contouring is almost impossible. If the anthropometry of male physique winners is unreliable (see Chapter 7), that of women beauty winners is almost non-existent. As a result women do not have access to the detailed standards which are available to men. The chest measurement is taken just below the breasts. The waist and calf are taped in the same way as for men. The hips are measured around the largest part, where they are the broadest and the buttocks are the deepest. There seems to be a concensus among gymnasia owners worling with beauty contestants that the bust and hip measurements should be the same and the waist should be approximately 12 inches smaller than either. Some say that the calf should be the same girth as the knee. There appears to be general agreement that most untrained American women tend to have oversized waists and thighs and underdeveloped calves.

Measure the girth of the knees and calves of a number of your friends. What do you conclude regarding the need for calf exercises? What exercises would you suggest?

The raw material which the average American female had at her disposal at the time "Norma" (fig. 6.2) was sculptured is shown in Table 6.2. It is evident that the ankle measurement was not taken as described on page 65. Probably it was taken directly around the ankle bones, and is therefore not comparable with the figures given for the Mr. Americas. For comparative purposes the average figures of 37 Miss Americas are shown in the same table. How reliable they are cannot be determined. They rather clearly support the opinion that the typical American girl tends to be much too large in the waist and hips. They also indicate that Miss America winners tend to be taller and more slender than the average woman.

TABLE 6.2.   ANTHROPOMETRY OF SELECTED AMERICAN WOMEN

	"Norma"	Average of 37 Miss Americas
Height	5'3.5"	5'7"
Bust	35.5"	34.7"
Waist	29"	24.1"
Hips	39"	35.2"
Thigh	20"	
Calf	13"	
Ankle	9.5"	
Weight	120-135 lbs.	120 lbs.

Fig. 6.2.   "Norma," the average 18 year old American girl of a few years ago. Modelled by Abram Belskie under the direction of Dr. Robert Latou Dickinson. (Courtesy of the American Museum of Natural History.)

REFERENCES

1. Shirley Ann Chew. A Study of the Use of Weights in Restrictive Exercises for Girls in Corrective Physical Education. Unpublished Masters Project, University of Southern California, 1960.
2. Jack R. Leighton. Weight Lifting—for Girls, *Journal of Health, Physical Education, Recreation*, XXXI:19-20, May-June, 1960.
3. Albert R. Behnke and Jack Wilmore. *Evaluation and Regulation of Body Build and Composition*. Englewood Cliffs: Prentice-Hall, Inc., 1974, pp. 127 and 129.
4. Jack H. Wilmore. Alterations in strength, body composition and anthropometric measurements consequent to a 10-weeks weight training program, *Medicine and Science in Sports*, 6:133-138, Summer 1974.
5. J. L. Mayhew and D. M. Gross. Body Composition Changes in Young Women with High Resistance Weight Training, *Research Quarterly*, 45:433-440, December, 1974.
6. Christina McIntyre. Effect of a Weight Training Program on Body Contours of Young Women 18-22. Unpublished Masters Thesis, University of California at Los Angeles, 1967.
7. Sandra Price. The Effects of Weight Training on Strength, Endurance, Girth, and Body Composition in College Women. Unpublished Masters Thesis, Brigham Young University, 1974.
8. C. Rosenthal. Physiology of Massage. In *Handbook of Physical Therapy*. Chicago: American Medical Association, 1939, p. 78.
9. Vernon Hernlund and Arthur H. Steinhaus. Do Mechanical Vibrators Take Off or Redistribute Fat? *Journal of the Association for Physical and Mental Rehabilitation*, 11:96, May-June, 1967.
10. American College of Sports Medicine. Position Statement on the Use and Abuse of Anabolic-Androgenic Steroids in Sports, *sports medicine bulletin*, 13:1 *et seq.*, January, 1978.

On taking
measurements

7

Weight trainers are quite likely to talk of the value of exercise for health and physical fitness but to be interested primarily in the girth of their muscles. There is probably no type of recording in the entire field of physical activity so subject to exaggeration, not to say downright mendacity, as the physical measurements of body builders. He who believes everything he hears and reads about the measurements of physique competitors is credulous indeed. One should look with great suspicion upon the alleged measurements of any contestant who is not willing to have them taken by competent anthropometrists. It is strange indeed that the Mr. America anthropometric data have been permitted to rest upon nothing better than the word of the men concerned—some of whom have proved uncooperative—whereas a lifter is required to use weights checked and certified by competent weighers using tested scales.

There are standard techniques for taking anthropometric measurements, and they must be followed exactly by anyone not deliberately desiring to deceive himself and others. It is necessary that all measuring be done by a second person as it is almost impossible for a man to measure himself and be sure that the tape does not slant up, down, or sideways. Measurements must be taken BEFORE, not AFTER, exercise. The data desired are the normal sizes, not the temporary girths of muscles swollen by vigorous activity. A flexible steel tape should be used, preferably one marked off in tenths of an inch rather than in the usual sixteenths. The tape is laid on the skin and pulled snug but not tight. If too loose, it will give figures which are too large; if pulled so tightly as to cut into the flesh, it will give readings which are too small. Be certain that no fingers are under the tape. This warning may seem ludicrous, but it is not an unusual situation when the circumference of the chest is being determined. Actually both sides of the body should be measured and reported, but it is the general custom to give only one figure—

which, of course, may be assumed to be the one more favorable to the individual in question. Height must be taken barefoot and weight in the nude.

There is no such thing as an "official" set of prescribed measurements, but most of the recommendations made by Willoughby[1] about thirty-five years ago have been generally accepted and comprise the present practice. Instructions for the measurements ordinarily reported in male physique contests are as follows:

Neck—The head is erect, eyes looking forward, neck muscles relaxed. The measurement is made at the smallest girth, just above the Adam's apple.

Upper arm—The arm is raised to shoulder height and the elbow flexors are fully contracted, palm down, fist clenched and turned down. The girth is taken at the point of greatest size of the biceps. The tape must be at right angls to the upper arm bone (humerus).

Forearm—The arm is straight, with no bend at the wrist, and held at an angle away from the body. The fist is clenched so that the forearm muscles are fully contracted. The taping is made below the elbow at the point of greatest girth.

Wrist—The palm is held up, fingers extended in line with the forearm. The measurement is made at the point between the base of the hand and the bony protuberance on the little finger side of the hand (styloid process of the ulna).

Chest normal—The body is erect, the head up, breathing normal. The circumference is taken at the largest part. The tape is placed just above the nipples in front and must be straight across the back. The measurer must check carefully to make sure that the subject is not contracting the latissimus dorsi.

Chest expanded—The tape is kept in the same position as for Chest Normal while the subject inhales deeply and expands his chest to its greatest size. Again, care must be taken to see that he does not flex the latissimus dorsi in the process. One occasionally sees advertisements claiming that someone has a chest expansion of ten inches or so and can develop the same amount in those who take his course. Expansions of this kind are not typical of the experienced weight trainer. If the expanded chest measurement of such an individual exceeds the normal chest measurement by more than two or three inches, it must be carefully rechecked as the tape has probably slipped or muscle contraction has been included. Neither is there the slightest evidence that increasing the chest expansion in this manner will double one's life expectancy, as is often claimed.

Waist—The body is erect, the abdominal muscles in a normal state of tonus. The waist is measured at the smallest part, usually a little above the navel. The abdomen must not be sucked in, although figures are often cited which suggest very strongly that this is exactly what has occurred.

Thigh—The body is erect, feet about six inches apart, weight equally distributed on each foot, and thigh muscles relaxed. Measurement is made at the largest part, usually just below the buttocks.

Calf—The body is erect, with heels on the floor, the weight equally distributed on each foot. The measurement is taken at the largest girth.

Ankle—The body is erect, with the heels on the floor and the weight equally distributed on each foot. Measurement is made at the smallest part, usually about two inches above the ankle bones (lateral and medial malleolus).

In the present craze for sheer bulk, body builders frequently lose sight of the fact that the individual measurements must be in proportion if the result is to be harmonious, that is, the potential physique contest winner must be not only well developed, but also symmetrical in appearance. For some reason they have concentrated on the image of huge arms. The results have often resulted in a disproportionate body development. More losers in physique contests suffer from the fact that their legs seem underdeveloped in comparison with their arms and upper body than from the other way around.

What is the average American male physique and what sort of development must he attain if he is to have a chance to win in topnotch competition? The answer to the first question will be found in Table 7.1. These figures date back to the 1940s and are quite incomplete, but are probably reasonably descriptive of the average young American male of today.

TABLE 7.1. ANTHROPOMETRY OF THE AVERAGE AMERICAN MALE

Height	68.5 in.
Weight	140-150 lbs.
Upper arm	10 in.
Chest normal	34 in.
Waist	30 in.
Thigh	20 in.
Calf	14 in.

How such an individual appears can be seen in figure 7.1, which is a photograph of the statue of "Norman" created by a sculptor working under the direction of Dr. Robert L. Dickson to depict the average American of that time. Norman's physique may be compared with that of the "ideal" as represented by the various Mr. Americas. The anthropometric data for the winners to date are given in Table 7.2, and a photograph of one of them, Bill Pearl, is reproduced in figure 7.2 for comparison with Norman. The contrast is startling, to say the least.

The authentic Mr. America contest is sponsored by the AAU. Judges are selected by the chairman of the National AAU Judges Committee and the meet chairman. Entrants are judged on the basis of:

Symmetry—the overall balance of body parts and muscle groups.

Muscularity—combination of muscle size, development, definition, and hardness.

Presentation—grooming, posture, carriage, projection, and posing ability.

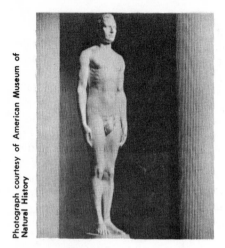

Photograph courtesy of American Museum of Natural History

Photograph courtesy of Pearl & Stern

Fig. 7.1.   Norman, the Average American Male of a Few Years Ago.

Fig. 7.2.   William Pearl, Mr. America 1953, Mr. Universe 1953, Professional Mr. Universe 1961 and 1967, who represents a present-day American male ideal.

In addition a lesser number of points are awarded at an interview held to determine the competitor's ability to communicate. A quirk in the rules provides "Employing drugs to increase athletic efficiency" constitutes grounds for disqualification,[2] although, oddly enough, the competitors are not required to demonstrate any sort of athletic ability.

At the time of the inception of these contests, the competitors were largely weight lifters, and Mr. Americas like John Grimek and Steve Stanko were champion lifters as well as physique competition winners. As time went on, it became evident that the type of body build which wins the physique contests is markedly different from that typical of the champion weight lifters. The physique winner tends to have comparatively small bones, joints, waist, hips, and buttocks, combined with broad shoulders and a huge chest (fig. 7.3). The lifter is likely to have comparatively big bones, a relatively long trunk, short arms and legs, a thick waist, and well-developed buttocks (fig. 7.4). Merited Master of Sport Vasily Alexeyev (fig. 7.4), the World's Strongest Man, is 6' 1" tall, weighs 355 pounds, has a 59 inch chest (expanded), a 63 inch waist, and a 22 inch neck!

Study the anthropometry of the average American male and of the Mr. Americas. What parts of the body of the former are most in need of development?

| **Fig. 7.3** | **Figure 7.4** | **Figure 7.5** |

Fig. 7.3. Steve Reeves, 1947 Mr. America. Many fans still consider Reeves to have been the greatest example of the **V** shape in the history of physique contests. (Courtesy **Iron Man Magazine.**)

Fig. 7.4 Vasily Alexeyev (USSR), 1972 Olympic Superheavyweight Weight Lifting Champion. This great lifter exemplifies the barrellike physique characteristics of the giants of strength. He is 6'1" tall and weighs 330 lbs. Alexeyev holds sixty-nine world's weight lifting records. (Courtesy **Iron Man Magazine.**)

Fig. 7.5. Chris Dickerson. Mr. USA 1968, Amateur Mr. Universe 1973, Professional Mr. Universe 1974. In 1970 Dickerson made history by becoming the first black to achieve Mr. America honors.

Fig. 7.6. John C. Grimek, Mr. America 1940-41, Mr. USA 1948, Mr. Universe, and considered by many authorities to possess the most perfect male physique of all time, is a former National and North American Weight Lifting Champion. He was a member of the 1936 Olympic team and represented the United States in the World Weight Lifting Championships in 1938. This athlete competed in both the light heavyweight and the heavyweight divisions. He has held various national records. His left-hand clean and jerk as a heavyweight still stands.

Figure 7.6

Some of the earlier Mr. Americas were outstanding athletes (fig. 8.1), but the trend has been steadily away from performance and toward display. Champion weight lifters no longer win Mr. America contests, and Mr. Americas do not win weight lifting championships, although, of course, Mr. Americas may demonstrate great strength when the amounts of weight used in their training exercises are taken as the criteria (fig. 7.7).

Fig. 7.7.   Val Vasilieff, Mr. America 1964, in a relaxed pose rather than in a tensed pose, as usually assumed by physique contestants. Willoughby (in **The Super Athletes,** p. 167) credits Vasilieff with a correct two-hands curl of 220 pounds, a press of 315 pounds, a snatch of 270 pounds, a clean and jerk of 360 pounds, a bench press of 450 pounds, and a two-hands dead lift of 600 pounds—rather convincing evidence that shapeliness and strength may be combined.

A further word of explanation about the Mr. America title might clarify the picture for the newcomer to the field of weight training. Apparently the title is not copyrighted, and the idea of using it occurred independently to two entrepreneurs in 1939. In connection with the AAU weight-lifting championships in Chicago that year a board of artists and other aesthetes selected the handsome but underdeveloped Roland Essmaker as Mr. America. That same year Bert Goodrich, a worthy choice, was awarded the same title in an Amsterdam, New York, contest. In 1940 competition was held on a truly national basis and was won by John C. Grimek. When he repeated his triumph the following year and appeared likely to continue to do so indefinitely, a rule was passed prohibiting a winner from competing in future contests. The men officially recognized as titleholders by the Amateur Athletic Union are listed in Table 7.2.

As interest in the event increased, some of the professional wrestlers took to calling themselves Mr. America, although they had no legitimate claim to

Year		Height	Weight	Neck	Chest, normal	Chest, expanded	Arm	Forearm	Wrist	Waist	Thigh	Calf	Ankle
1940-41	John C. Grimek	5'8.50"	195	18.00	49.70	50.70	18.70	14.50	7.70	31.00	27.00	17.70	10.00
1942	Frank Leight	5'11.25"	209	17.00	46.90	49.50	17.00	15.00	7.95	32.00	25.00	15.00	10.25
1943	Jules Bacon	5'7"	178	16.50	46.10	**47.60**	16.60	12.70	7.00	29.00	25.00	15.70	8.60
1944	Steve Stanko	5'11.50"	203	17.50	48.50	50.00	18.50	13.40	7.95	30.00	28.00	16.75	10.00
1945	Clarence Ross	5'9.50"	190	16.75	47.25	**48.80**	17.30	13.50	7.50	32.00	25.30	16.10	9.00
1946	Alan Stephan	5'11.50"	205	17.50	48.50	50.25	18.10	14.50	7.50	31.50	26.00	17.00	10.50
1947	Steve Reeves	6'1"	213	17.50	49.50	51.00	18.00	**14.50**	7.50	29.00	25.50	17.75	9.30
1948	George Eiferman	5'8"	200	17.25	47.50	50.00	18.00	13.25	7.25	32.00	24.50	16.00	9.75
1949	Jack Delinger	5'8"	205	18.00	50.00	52.00	19.00	14.25	8.00	31.00	26.50	17.25	10.00
1950	John Farbotnik	5'9"	195	17.00	50.00	51.00	18.00	**14.50**	7.25	32.00	25.50	16.25	**9.00**
1951	Roy S. Hilligenn	5'6"	178	17.50	48.50	**50.50**	17.75	14.50	7.50	31.00	24.50	16.25	8.00
1952	James Park	5'9"	187	**17.50**	49.00	**50.50**	18.60	**14.50**	**7.70**	30.00	24.50	17.00	**9.50**
1953	William Pearl	5'11.25"	193	17.62	48.25	50.00	18.00	15.00	7.25	32.50	24.50	16.75	9.50
1954	Richard DuBois	6'1"	225	18.00	50.00	52.00	18.50	15.00	8.00	32.25	26.50	17.00	**9.90**
1955	Steve D. Klisanin	5'10"	185	17.00	47.00	49.00	18.00	14.50	7.75	31.00	25.00	17.00	11.00
1956	Ray Schaefer	5'10"	202	**17.00**	**47.20**	**48.70**	**17.80**	**14.00**	**7.60**	**31.75**	24.50	**16.20**	**9.35**
1957	Ronald Lacy	5'9"	185	17.00	47.00	49.50	17.00	13.50	7.25	30.00	24.50	17.00	9.10
1958	Tom Sansone*	5'11"	212	17.50	49.50	52.00	19.25	15.50	7.75	31.50	26.00	17.50	10.00
1959	Harry Johnson	5'8.75"	185	16.75	45.00	47.50	16.90	13.00	7.75	30.00	26.00	16.00	9.25
1960	Lloyd Lerille	5'6"	180	16.75	47.50	50.50	17.12	13.25	8.00	31.00	24.00	16.25	9.00
1961	Ray Routledge	6'	200	17.50	50.00	51.00	18.50	16.00	8.00	32.00	26.50	17.50	9.50
1962	Joe Abbenda	6'	205	17.50	49.50	51.00	18.25	14.75	7.25	32.00	25.50	16.25	9.00
1963	Vern Weaver	5'9.50"	205	17.50	49.50	51.00	18.75	13.50	7.75	32.00	26.00	17.25	9.50
1964	Val Vasilieff	5'11"	210	18.00	52.00	54.00	19.00	16.50	8.35	30.00	27.00	18.00	10.00
1965	Jerry Daniels	6'0.25"	224	18.00	49.25	51.00	18.75	14.50	7.50	32.50	26.50	17.00	10.50
1966	Bob Gajda	5'9.50"	200	19.00	47.00	48.50	18.50	14.50	7.50	28.00	25.00	18.50	10.75
1967	Dennis Tinerino	6'1"	220	18.00	50.00	53.00	19.50	15.00	7.50	33.00	27.00	18.00	10.50
1968	James Haislop	5'11.50"	222	18.00	50.00	51.50	19.00	14.50	7.25	31.00	27.50	18.25	9.50
1969	Boyer Coe	5'8"	210	**17.85**	**49.50**	**51.00**	**19.00**	**14.75**	**7.95**	**33.30**	**25.70**	**17.00**	**9.60**
1970	Chris Dickerson	5'6"	188	17.50	47.50	49.50	18.00	14.00	7.75	32.00	25.25	18.00	9.50
1971	Casey Viator	5'8"	217	**18.10**	50.00	**51.50**	19.36	**15.00**	**8.05**	31.50	28.00	18.00	**10.00**
1972	Steve Michalik	5'10"	215	**17.75**	50.00	**51.00**	19.00	**14.75**	**7.90**	28.00	27.00	18.00	**9.75**
1973	James Morris	5'11"	221	17.50	49.00	50.50	19.25	17.00	7.75	32.00	25.50	17.00	9.50
1974	Ron Thompson												
1975	Dale Adrian	5'7.5"	198	17.50	49.00	52.00	19.25	15.00	7.12	30.00	26.00	18.00	9.75
1976	Kalman Szkalak	5'10"	210	**17.60**	**48.25**	**50.25**	20.12	**14.50**	**7.85**	30.00	27.00	17.50	**9.65**
1977	Dave Johns	5'10"	232	**18.00**	**54.00**	**56.00**	21.50	**17.00**	7.75	**28.50**	29.00	19.00	9.50

*Deceased October 16, 1975

Note: Physical measurements of body builders are often exaggerated. Most of these data were obtained from the Mr. Americas themselves, but accuracy cannot be guaranteed. Figures in bold are estimates made by David P. Willoughby as a result of the failure of the subject to supply the necessary data.

this designation. Eventually, ambitious promoters organized rival groups such as the International Federation of Body Builders (IFBB) and the World Body Building Guild, awarded this same title to the winners, and began publicizing them accordingly in their magazines. This has been the source of a great deal of confusion. Starting in 1977, however, amateurs from the IFBB have been permitted to participate in the AAU Mr. America competitions and vice versa. Possibly this will eventually result in a single Mr. America. The men listed in Table 7.2 are the only ones recognized by the AAU as authorized to use this title. They should not be confused with the winners of the Mr. USA title.

Probably the most prestige is attached to the winning of one of the shows produced in London by the National Amateur Body Builders Association (NABBA), the largest organization of its kind. In spite of its name the NABBA does not have the backing of any amateur association. Originally both amateurs and professionals competed against each other, but in 1952 separate classes for each were introduced. It has been declared an outlaw by the international amateur body, The Federation International Halterophile et Culturiste. Whether amateur standing is of any particular value to a physique contestant who has little or no interest in entering weight-lifting meets or other amateur athletic events is questionable. The NABBA and the IFBB have continued to attract a sizeable array of famed body builders. The picture is further confused by the fact that the British Weight Lifting Association, the IFBB, and other promoters have sponsored shows at which they awarded the title Mr. Universe to the winner. The situation is analogous to that in professional wrestling where a man may be a "World Champion" on his own circuit and almost completely unknown elsewhere.

Curiously enough, the Soviets strongly encourage weight lifting but violently denounce body building as "alien to the Soviet notion of physical education." They portray body building as a Western creation which originated in England and then spread to the United States.

Would you consider the typical Mr. America an athlete? Justify your answer.

It is, of course, totally unrealistic for the average man to hope to attain the measurements claimed by the Mr. Americas. A much more rational approach is for him to set as his goal attainment of a physique which is both well developed and well balanced, even if not as massive as that of physique contest winners. On the basis of over fifty years of observation and study of well-developed athletes and body builders, the noted anthropometrist and historian of weight training David P. Willoughby has devised a chart on which an individual can plot his measurements and determine the symmetry of his body. With this information available, he can determine at a glance what parts require specialized training and evaluate the results of such training over short or long periods of time. Table 7.3 is a considerably abridged form of the Willoughby Chart.

Status of Ratio or Measurement →

	Minimum		Small						Medium			Large								Maximum	
Weight ÷ Height	1.6	1.7	1.8	1.9	2.0	2.1	2.2	2.3	2.4	2.5	2.6	2.7	2.8	2.9	3.0	3.1	3.2	3.3	3.4	3.5	3.6
Neck	13.0			14.0					15.0			16.0		17.0		18.0			19.0		
Biceps, R.	12.1		13.0			14.0			15.0			16.0		17.0				18.0			
,, L.	12.0		13.0			14.0			15.0			16.0				17.0			18.0		
Forearm, R.	10.1			11.0				12.0			13.0				14.0				15.0		
,, L.	10.0			11.0				12.0			13.0				14.0				15.0		
Wrist, R.		6.0			6.5			7.0				7.5			8.0				8.5		
,, L.			6.0		6.5			7.0			7.5				8.0			8.5			
Chest (normal)		34.0	35.0	36.0	37.0	38.0	39.0	40.0	41.0	42.0	43.0	44.0	45.0	46.0	47.0	48.0		49.0		50.0	51.0
Waist		25.0	26.0	27.0	28.0	29.0	30.0	31.0	32.0	33.0		34.0		35.0		36.0		37.0		38.0	
Hips	30.0	31.0	32.0	33.0	34.0	35.0	36.0	37.0		38.0	39.0	40.0	41.0	42.0		43.0		44.0	45.0		46.0
Thigh, R.		18.0	19.0		20.0	21.0	22.0	23.0		24.0		25.0		26.0			27.0				
,, L.		18.0	19.0		20.0	21.0	22.0	23.0		24.0		25.0		26.0			27.0				
Knee, R.		12.0		13.0			14.0			15.0		16.0		17.0				18.0			
,, L.		12.0		13.0			14.0			15.0		16.0		17.0				18.0			
Calf, R.		12.0	13.0			14.0			15.0			16.0		17.0			18.0				
,, L.		12.0	13.0			14.0			15.0			16.0		17.0			18.0				
Ankle, R.	7.0		7.5		8.0			8.5		9.0			9.5		10.0			10.5			
,, L.	7.0		7.5		8.0			8.5		9.0			9.5		10.0			10.5			

(Girths)

Instructions: Make the required measurements according to the directions given earlier in chapter 5 and plot the data on the appropriate scales by making heavy dots at the proper points. Plot the larger of the two arms as the right arm, regardless of whether it is actually the right or the left, and vice versa. Connect the dots by means of a heavy line. The more nearly this coincides with a line drawn perpendicularly from the Weight/Height point to the bottom of the chart, the more symmetrical are the proportions of the body. A variation of ±2.5 percent is acceptable. To help in visualizing these limits, parallel lines may be drawn at 1.05 and 0.95 percent of the Weight/Height figure. In obese individuals body weight will take care of itself if the oversized areas, particularly the waist, are brought into line with the other girth measurements, particularly the wrists and ankles. (Copyright by David P. Willoughby. Reproduced by special permission.)

REFERENCES

1. David P. Willoughby. *How to Take Your Measurements*. (Montreal: Your Physique Publishing Co., 1944).
2. *Official AAU Physique Handbook*. (Indianapolis: Amateur Athletic Union of the United States, 1977, p. 16.

Weight
training for athletes

8

Writing in the purest academese, Jeffress and Peter have stated, "In our view the teleological significance of any response to overloading lies in its contribution to increasing the capacity of the animal to perform."[1] What they mean is that the value of muscular development depends upon what you can do with it. Yet there are few questions in the field of physical training which are more controversial than the relationship between increases in strength and gains in performance. For every thesis or published study reporting that the practice of progressive resistance exercises improved performance in swimming, running, jumping, or some other activity there is another stating that no such benefits could be observed. Pierson and Rasch were forced to conclude:

> The role of strength in motor performance is not clear, the effect of strength development in conditioning to the rigors of an activity is conjectural, and the evidence concerning the relationships of strength, body size, and composition is contradictory.[2]

Obviously a certain amount of strength is necessary for successful participation in any sport. Once this level is reached, further gains in strength do not appear to be accompanied by equivalent increases in performance. The optimal strength levels for various forms of activity are not known, however, and it is probably safe to assume that most athletes will profit by developing more than they have (fig. 8.1). The practice of a sport only improves strength up to the amount required to execute the basic movements of that activity. It is necessary for the athlete to pursue a program specifically designed to increase strength if he is to get stronger. The training programs which follow have been selected with a view to showing what is actually being done in certain fields of athletics today. They will serve to give the reader some idea of what those most closely connected with these sports be-

Fig. 8.1.   Ronald Lacy, Mr. America and Most Muscular 1957. Lacy attended college on a football scholarship and earned letters in three sports.

lieve best meet their needs, but they should not be blindly accepted nor assumed to constitute some sort of an argument against personal experimentation.

Football

Of all the professional developers of competitive athletes the football coaches seem to have been the most progressive in incorporating weight training into their conditioning programs. So far as the writer has been able to determine, the most comprehensive procedure of this type is that employed by the University of Texas. It is considerably more elaborate than it is practical to present here, but the following description will at least give a good idea of its major facets.

Like many other coaches, the Longhorns are partial to circuit training because of the cardiorespiratory benefits believed to result from its use. The circuit used by them during the end of the football season and the beginning of spring practice includes the following stations: (1) standing press; (2) upright rowing motion; (3) squat jump (maximum number in 15 seconds); (4) bent-over rowing motion; (5) bench press; (6) stair climb, using two 20-inch steps (maximum number in 1 minute); (7) parallel bar dip (maximum number); (8) barbell curl; (9) dead lift and shoulder shrug; (10) sit-ups on incline board (maximum number in 25 seconds with board at a 30-degree angle); (1) knee extension-flexion.

The athlete is tested to determine the maximum load with which he can accomplish three repetitions of each of the barbell exercises. He is then assigned weights 20 to 30 per cent of this figure and timed to determine how long it takes him to complete three laps around the circuit without any rest pauses between stations or laps. Next he is assigned a target time about one-third less than this figure. When he can complete the circuit in the target time, the work load is increased, the man is retested, and a new target time is established (fig. 8.2).

Between the end of spring training and the beginning of the summer vacation the players are placed on a regular barbell program stressing the development of strength. The schedule includes the following exercises: (1) standing press, (2) curl, (3) bent-over rowing, (4) upright rowing, (5) dead lift, (6) shoulder shrug, (7) bench press, (8) half-squat, (9) heel raise, (10) squat run—40 pounds for 8 seconds.

All exercises are performed for two sets, but the number of repetitions differs according to the position played.

A somewhat similar training program plus some isometric exercises and quarter-mile runs is followed during the summer vacation.[3]

For many schools and colleges such a program would be too elaborate to be practical. They might prefer the more conventional program followed by Louisiana State University:

Exercise	Sets	Repetitions
Clean and press	4	6
Pull-up to waist	4	4
Squat	4	8
Bench press	4	8
Dead lifts	4	6

Kloppenburg[4] prefers the variable resistance apparatus shown in figure 4.9 (p. 44) and has his players perform two sets of the following exercises three times each week, emphasizing the use of weights which require an all-out effort:

Exercise	Repetitions
Bench press	5
Heel raise	12
Leg press	12
Standing press	5
Latissimus machine	5
Triceps extension	5
Cleans	5
Curls	5
Reverse curls	5

Fig. 8.2. University of Texas Football Players Training with the Weights. The man on the right is Tommy Nobis, All-American and All-Professional guard.

The Los Angeles Rams have their players train for maximal strength during the off season. During the season they train twice a week, using 60 per cent of their maximum to maintain their strength. Bench presses, curls, shoulder shrugs, and squats are emphasized.

The weak spot in all of the foregoing programs seems to be the lack of neck exercises. The frequency of neck injuries in football is often blamed on the fragility of the first and second cervical vertebrae. It seems an elementary precaution to strengthen the muscles guarding this vulnerable area.

Medical authorities believe that it is important to maintain a strength ratio of 60/40 between the knee extensors and flexors. Some trainers argue that if the ratio reaches 70/30 hamstring pulls become almost a certainty. This implies that conditioning programs should pay more attention to strengthening the hamstrings than is usually the case.

Baseball

The case for the use of weight training in baseball and the principles to be followed in devising such a regimen have been impressively presented by Stallings.[5] Those considering introducing such a program will find his discussion decidedly informative.

Perhaps the program which has received the greatest acceptance among baseball players is that presented by Wickstrom.[6] The exercises, with the proposed starting weights for each, follow:

(1) clean and press—one-third body weight plus 10 pounds, (2) straight-arm pull-overs—one-quarter body weight minus 5 pounds, (3) sit-ups—with hands behind the head and no weight, (4) supine press—one-half body weight (5) bent-over lateral raise—10 to 15 pounds dumbbells, (6) half-squats—one-half body weight, (7) ulnar flexion of wrist—5 pounds, and (8) wrist curl—35 pounds. Wickstrom suggests two or three sets of five to seven repetitions

each, with three to five minutes of rest between each set. He believes that this schedule should be used three times a week for off-season or preseason conditioning.

Edwards[7] has worked out a set of movements specific for baseball. They include: (1) trunk rotation—arms held out to the sides on line with the shoulders, a six-to-ten-pound dumbbell in each hand; body twisted as far as possible to one side and then to the other; (2) one-hand swing—an eight-or-ten-pound dumbbell held at the opposite shoulder and swung across the chest as if batting; (3) wrist curls—done standing with the forearms parallel to the ground; (4) triceps extension; (5) wrist abductor.

Basketball

In spite of the fact that it was originally published several years ago, the O'Connor and Sills[8] program seems to have retained favor among basketball players. They especially recommend it for preseason training, although suggesting that it may be continued during the season: (1) wrist curls, (2) curls, (3) side raises with dumbbells, (4) presses, (5) forward raise with dumbbells, (6) heel raise, (7) walking squats with barbell on shoulders. They propose ten to twelve repetitions of each arm exercise and two sets of ten to twelve repetitions for the legs.

Burnham[9] offers a training schedule especially designed to develop rebounding ability: (1) Military press, (2) erect rowing, (3) bent rowing, (4) two-arm curl, (5) running in place with twenty-pound jacket in half-squat position, (6) stair step, (7) heel raise. The barbell exercises are to be done in three sets of eight to twelve repetitions each. Running in place is performed for five sets of ten seconds each.

Judo

The following program is used by students of judo who attend the Kodokan.[10] It is of particular interest because of its stress on the use of dumbbells. Perhaps this has resulted from the fact that Japanese studies have shown that the top judoka were lacking in back and arm strength. The exercises include: (1) squat, (2) dumbbell straight-arm pull-over (3) heel raise, (4) dumbbell press on bench, (5) flying motion, (6) dumbbell rowing, (7) barbell curl, (8) standing barbell triceps extension, (9) seated dumbbell press behind neck, (10) sit-ups.

A number of alternate programs are presented by Ishikawa and Draeger.[11] These experts recommend that a schedule of three sets of ten repetitions each be followed.

Swimming

Weight training has been popular with swimming coaches ever since Bob Kiphuth introduced it at Yale in 1936. One study[12] has shown that of 106 swimming coaches who responded to a questionnaire 67 per cent used weight training programs in training their swimmers. Of the 33 per cent who did not, 60 per cent would have done so if equipment and facilities had been available.

Homola[13] has devised a series of exercises specifically designed to develop the muscles and flexibility desirable in this sport. He emphasizes that they must be performed through the full range of movement. His program consists of the following: (1) pull down on a lat machine, (2) bent over rowing motion, (3) dumbbell extensions, lateral raises, and rowing motions while prone on a bench, (4) squats, (5) stiff arm and bent arm pullovers, (6) supine lateral raises on a bench, (7) decline bench presses, (8) iron boot alternate leg raises while supine on an incline bench, and backward raises while prone, (9) isometric scissors exercise against a partially inflated inner tube, (10) donkey toe raises, (11) stiff-leg deadlifts, and (12) side bends with a dumbbell. He suggests eight to ten repetitions and working up from a single set to three sets. Two or three exercise periods a week are recommended.

Tennis

For some reason the use of weight training exercises to improve tennis playing ability has received little attention. Lew Hoad,[14] however, gives it a good deal of credit for his success. He prefers six exercises, all done with a dumbbell: (1) wrist curls, (2) reverse wrist curls, (3) dumbbell is held with the hand in the midposition. The weight is extended to the right as far as possible and then to the left as far as possible. This is a variation of the wrist curl exercise. (4) Curl. (5) Weight is held horizontally out in front. After a few seconds it is raised to the vertical position. The dumbbell is then returned to the horizontal position. Hoad prefers ten repetitions of each exercise, using as much weight as one can handle. It must be recognized that this is a highly specialized program, not one designed for the person who needs to increase overall muscular strength and power.

Track and Field

Track and field events are so varied that it is difficult to prescribe a general program that will meet the needs of competitors in each event. Berger,[15] however, offers the following off-season program: (1) curl, (2) bench press, (3) one-third squat, (4) upright rowing, (5) sit-up, (6) leg curl with iron boot, (7) forward bend with barbell behind neck, (8) heel raise, (9) press, (10) side bend with barbell on shoulders, (11) wrist curl, (12) knee extension in seated position. He does not recommend this for use during the season as he believes that the fatigue which results from its practice may distract from the development of sports skills.

Weight training is especially popular among the weight throwers. Gary Gubner in effect had a choice of participating in the 1964 Olympic Games as a shot-putter or as a weight lifter and Al Feuerbach was the AAU shot put and weight lifting champion in 1974. The following program was used by Jay Silvester, the best combined shot-put and discus thrower in the world: (1) clean and jerk, (2) dead lift, (3) bench press, (4) jumping squats, (5) lateral raises on an incline board, (6) triceps extension, (7) press on an incline board, (8) sit-ups. His program was of the light and heavy variety. He lifted three days a week during the off-season and two or three days a week during the competitive season.

John P. Jesse, who has had considerable success working with weight throwers and other athletes in Southern California, believes that training programs for the former should stress the development of power in the hamstrings, lower back, abdomen, serratus anterior, hands, and fingers. In his opinion too many weight throwers make the mistake of attempting to gain tremendous overall strength while actually neglecting the muscles most important for success in their particular sport.

Wrestling

Unlike football and swimming coaches, wrestling experts have tended to be more or less skeptical of the benefits of weight training for the amateur grappler. This may be because they believe the body building effects of this form of exercise make it more difficult for the wrestler to "make weight." However, Bill Farrell, coach of the highly successful 1972 United States Olympic Wrestling Team, considers that his emphasis on weight training was one of the principal reasons why his team was so outstanding. He employed an earlier version of the machine shown in figure 4.9 (p. 44). The wrestlers performed three circuits three days a week, working at 75 to 80 per cent of maximum. He suggests that this program be performed only twice a week during the wrestling season, preferably at least two to three hours before practice.

Van Vliet[16] has proposed an out of season weight training program for high school wrestlers. He recommends the following exercises: (1) sit ups

Fig. 8.3.   Lloyd "Red" Lerille, Mr. America 1960. Lerille was undefeated during three seasons of high school wrestling and was runner-up in the All-Navy championships before deciding to devote his full attention to body building.

with weight held behind head, (2) two arm reverse curl, (3) high pull up, (4) bench press, (5) straight arm pull downs, (6) leg press (squat may be substituted if leg press machine not available), (7) press, (8) bent over rowing, (9) dead lift, (10) two arm curl, (11) bridge, holding weight on chest, (12) bent arm pull over. The wrestlers should start with eight repetitions and work up to fifteen. He should train three times a week and perform three sets of each exercise, according to Van Vliet.

Figure 8.3 shows an individual who has been highly successful both as a wrestler and a Mr. America. Bill Pearl (fig. 7.2) was also a wrestler while serving in the Navy.

Weight training programs advocated for athletes have differed from sport to sport and from coach to coach. What do you see as the basic principle that should underlie the choice of exercises for a particular athletic event? What research relating to weight training and athletic performance is still needed?

Summary

The point to be remembered is that the more closely a weight-training movement simulates an actual movement of the sport, the more helpful it is likely to be. An example might be the use of a dumbbell with the weight at one end (p. 50) used to strengthen the forearm and wrist of a tennis player. The reader can design his own program by determining which muscles are the most important in a given sport and then using the Muscle Chart (pp. 84-86) as a guide to effective exercises for those muscles. Those preferring more detailed information are referred to a booklet published by the University of Nebraska.[17] This provides a training schedule for both male and female athletes in nearly every intercollegiate sport.

REFERENCES

1. Robert N. Jeffress and James B. Peter. "Adaptations of Skeletal Muscle to Overloading—A Review," *Bulletin Los Angeles Neurological Society*, 35:134-144, July, 1970.
2. William R. Pierson and Philip J. Rasch. "Strength Development and Performance Capacity," *Journal of the Association for Physical and Mental Rehabilitation*, 17 et seq., January-February, 1963.
3. Terry Todd. "Progressive Resistance for Football at the University of Texas," *Strength & Health*, 32-18 et seq., 1964.
4. Bob Kloppenberg. "Conditioning for Football," *Athletic Journal*, 54:44 et seq., February, 1974.
5. Jack Stallings. "The Case for Weight Training in Baseball," *Scholastic Coach*, 35:32 et seq., February, 1966.

6. Ralph L. Wickstrom. "Weight Training for Baseball," *Scholastic Coach*, 29:36 *et seq.*, March, 1960.
7. Donald K. Edwards. "A Strength Building Program for Baseball," *Athletic Journal*, 45:12 *et seq.*, February, 1965.
8. Frank "Bucky" O'Connor and Frank Sills. "Heavy Resistance Exercises for Basketball Players," *Athletic Journal*, 36:6-8, June, 1956.
9. Stan Burnham. "Develop Your Rebounders with Weight Training," *Scholastic Coach*, 30 December, 1960.
10. Donn Draeger. "Weight Lifting for Judo," *Strength & Health*, June, 1960.
11. Takahiko Ishikawa and Donn E. Draeger. *Judo Training Methods: A Sourcebook*. Rutland, Vt.: Charles E. Tuttle Co., Inc., 1962, pp. 130-137.
12. Eric Riedel. "A Survey of Practices of Swimming Coaches Concerning Weight Training Programs." Unpublished Master's Thesis, Fresno State College, 1965.
13. Samuel Homola. "Weight Training for Speed Swimmers," *Swimming World*, 7:6 *et seq.*, January, 1966.
14. Lew Hoad. "Lew Hoad Tells You How to Put More Power in Your Game," *Tennis*, 11:63-65, September, 1975.
15. Richard A. Berger. "Strength Training for Track and Field," *Athletic Journal*, 43:50 *et seq.*, February, 1963.
16. George A. Van Vliet. "A Proposed Weight Training Program for High School Wrestlers." Unpublished Master's Thesis, University of Southern California, 1965.
17. Boyd Epley. *The Strength of Nebraska*. Lincoln: University of Nebraska, 1972.

Appendix 1: Superficial muscles of the human body

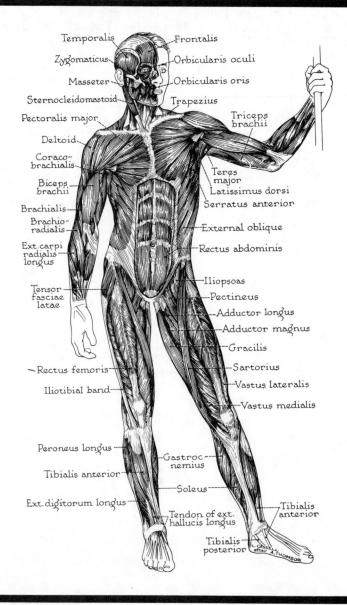

Temporalis
Frontalis
Zygomaticus
Orbicularis oculi
Masseter
Orbicularis oris
Sternocleidomastoid
Trapezius
Pectoralis major
Triceps brachii
Deltoid
Coraco-brachialis
Teres major
Biceps brachii
Latissimus dorsi
Serratus anterior
Brachialis
Brachio-radialis
External oblique
Ext. carpi radialis longus
Rectus abdominis
Iliopsoas
Tensor fasciae latae
Pectineus
Adductor longus
Adductor magnus
Gracilis
Rectus femoris
Sartorius
Iliotibial band
Vastus lateralis
Vastus medialis
Peroneus longus
Gastrocnemius
Tibialis anterior
Soleus
Ext. digitorum longus
Tibialis anterior
Tendon of ext. hallucis longus
Tibialis posterior

L. CASSELL after A. THOMSON

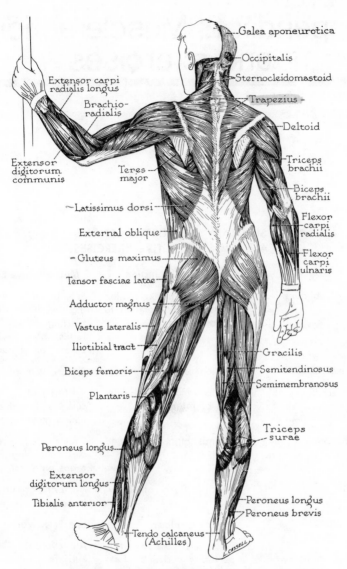

Galea aponeurotica
Occipitalis
Sternocleidomastoid
Trapezius
Deltoid
Extensor carpi radialis longus
Brachio-radialis
Triceps brachii
Biceps brachii
Extensor digitorum communis
Teres major
Flexor carpi radialis
Latissimus dorsi
External oblique
Flexor carpi ulnaris
Gluteus maximus
Tensor fasciae latae
Adductor magnus
Vastus lateralis
Iliotibial tract
Gracilis
Biceps femoris
Semitendinosus
Semimembranosus
Plantaris
Triceps surae
Peroneus longus
Extensor digitorum longus
Tibialis anterior
Peroneus longus
Peroneus brevis
Tendo calcaneus (Achilles)

L. CASSELL

Fig. A.2.   Superficial Muscles of the Human Body, Posterior View. From King, B. G., and Showers, J. J.: **Human Anatomy and Physiology.** Ed. 5. Philadelphia, W. B. Saunders Company, 1953.

Fig. A.1.   Superficial Muscles of the Human Body, Anterior View. From King, B. G., and Showers, M. J.: **Human Anatomy and Physiology.** Ed. 5. Philadelphia, W. B. Saunders Company, 1953.

Appendix 2: Muscle actions and exercises

SUMMARY OF MUSCLE ACTIONS AND MOST EFFECTIVE EXERCISES

Muscle	Principal Function	Most Effective Exercises
Abdominis obliquus	Flexion of trunk, flexion to same side, rotation to opposite side	Side bending while holding weight in one hand, twisting sit-ups and leg raises, body twists with barbell on shoulders
Abdominis rectus	Flexion of spine	Sit-ups, vee-ups
Biceps brachii	Flexion and inward rotation of forearm	All forms of curls, reverse curls, and supination-pronation movements
Biceps femoris	Extends thigh, flexes knee	Squats, leg press, leg curls, and leg backward raises with iron boot
Brachialis	Principal flexor of elbow	All forms of curls and reverse curls
Brachioradialis	Flexion of elbow	See Biceps brachii
Deltoid	Three-part muscle; part 1, performs horizontal flexion; part 2, abduction; part 3, horizontal extension	All overhead lifts, side and front raises
Erector spinae	Extension of trunk	Dead lifts, good morning exercise, swan exercise, side bends, dead lifts
Extensor carpi radialis	Extension and abduction of wrist	Reverse wrist curls, wrist abduction exercise

Muscle	Principal Function	Most Effective Exercises
Extensor carpi ulnaris	Extension and adduction of wrist	Reverse wrist curls, wrist adduction exercise
Flexor carpi radialis	Flexion and abduction of wrist	Wrist curls, wrist abduction exercise
Flexor carpi ulnaris	Flexion and adduction of wrist	Wrist curls, wrist adduction exercise
Gastrocnemius	Extends foot; aids in flexing knee	Heel raises, donkey raises in regular and inverted positions, walking on toes with barbell on shoulders
Gluteus maximus	Extension and outward rotation of thigh	Squat, backward leg extension with iron boot, outward rotation of leg with iron boot
Latissimus dorsi	Draws arms downward, backward, and inward	Lat machine, rowing motion, pull-over
Pectoralis major	Two-part muscle; part 1, functions in arm flexion and abduction; part 2, in arm extension and adduction	Pull-over, flying motion, bench press
Pronator quadratus	Pronates forearm	Pronation-supination of wrist
Quadriceps femoris	Extends knee	Squat, leg press, forward raise of leg, and seated knee extension with iron boot
Rectus femoris	Extends knee and flexes thigh; part of quadriceps femoris	See Quadriceps femoris
Rhomboids	Adduct scapula	Rowing motion, shoulder shrugs
Semimembranosus and semitendinosus (hamstrings)	Extends thigh and flexes knee	Squats, leg press, leg curls with iron boots, backward leg raises
Serratus anterior	Abduction of scapula	All overhead lifts, lateral raise, pull-over
Soleus	Extends foot	See Gastrocnemius
Sternocleidomastoid	Flexes and rotates head	Bridging, use of weights suspended from head strap

Muscle	Principal Function	Most Effective Exercises
Supinator	Supinates forearm	Supination-pronation exercise
Supraspinatus	Arm abduction	All overhead lifts, front and side raises
Teres major	Same as latissimus dorsi	See Latissimus dorsi
Trapezius	Elevates shoulders and abducts scapula	Shoulder shrugs, all overhead lifts, dead lifts
Triceps brachii	Extension of elbow joint	Overhead lifts, bench presses, French press
Vastus intermedius, internus, and medialis	Parts of quadriceps femoris	See Quadriceps femoris

Appendix 3: Glossary

Abduction. Movement away from the center line of the body.

Adduction. Movement toward the center line of the body.

Anabolic steroids. Synthetic hormones believed to promote growth of protein tissue.

Body composition. Fat weight + lean weight. Exercise decreases fat weight and increases lean weight, thus changing the percentage of each in the body.

Clean and jerk. An Olympic lift in which the weight is taken to the chest in one movement and then thrown overhead in a second movement.

Cuts. The separations seen between groups of muscle fibers in men in whom intensive training has produced a high degree of muscular definition.

Elastic rebound exercise. An exercise technique in which flexion is followed immediately by extension. The purpose is to use the elastic energy stored when stretching the contracted muscle. If there is a delay between flexion and extension this energy is lost as heat.

Endocrine glands. Glands which secrete a substance that affects another organ or part of the body.

Hormones. Chemical substances which can alter the functional activity of an organ of the body.

Hypertrophy. Enlargement in the size of a muscle. Increases in hypertrophy are not necessarily closely related to increases in strength.

Isokinetic. Constant motion; an isotonic contraction in which the speed of movement remains steady.

Isometric. Constant length; a contraction in which there is no apparent change in the angles of the bony levers.

Isotonic. Constant tension; a contraction in which the angles between the bony levers change.

Lean body weight.   Weight of the lean body mass, including water, mineral and organic substances. This is not fat-free weight, since it includes the weight of essential fat.

Negative exercise.   A form of isotonic exercise in which the muscle lengthens rather than shortens. Also called eccentric exercise.

Power clean.   An exercise in which a weight is taken from knee level to the shoulders in one movement.

Prone.   Face downward. The bench press is often erroneously termed the prone press. A true prone press would be a push-up.

Snatch.   An Olympic lift in which a weight is raised overhead in a single movement.

Sticking point.   The point in a lift at which the greatest effort is required in order to complete the movement. This occurs at the joint angle at which the mechanical efficiency is least advantageous.

Supine.   Face up.

Synergistic action.   Simultaneous contraction of two or more muscles to produce a desired action.

Appendix 4:
Selected references

The following list of suggested readings is presented for the guidance of the serious weight trainer who desires a more complete understanding of the scientific facts underlying his form of training. Articles cited in the text are not included here.

American College of Sports Medicine. Position Statement on the Recommended Quantity and Quality of Exercise for Developing and Maintaining Fitness in Healthy Adults. *sports medicine bulletin*, 13:1 et seq., July, 1978.

Anonymous, Organic Foods. *Food Technology*, 28:71-74, January 1974.

CLARKE, DAVID H. Adaptations in Strength and Muscular Endurance Resulting from Exercise. In Wilmore, Jack H., ed., *Exercise and Sport Sciences Review*. New York: Academic Press, 1973, I:73-102.

CLARKE, H. HARRISON. Isometric Versus Isotonic Exercises. *Physical Fitness Research Digest*, Series 1, July 1971.

———. Toward a Better Understanding of Muscular Strength. *Physical Fitness Research Digest*, Series 3, January, 1973.

———. Development of Muscular Strength and Endurance. *Physical Fitness Research Digest*, Series 4, January, 1974.

———. Strength Development and Motor-Sports Improvement. *Physical Fitness Research Digest*, Series 4, October, 1974.

GOLDING, LAWRENCE A. Drugs and Hormones. In Morgan, William P., ed., *Ergogenic Aids and Muscular Performance*. New York: Academic Press, 1972, pp. 367-397.

MUELLER, E. A. The Physiological Basis of Rest Pauses in Heavy Work. *Quarterly Journal of Experimental Physiology and Cognate Medical Sciences*, 38: 205-215, 1952.

MULLER, ERICH A. Influence of Training and of Inactivity on Muscle Strength. *Archives of Physical Medicine and Rehabilitation*, 51:449-462, August, 1970.

National Academy of Sciences, *Recommended Dietary Allowances*, 8th rev. ed. Washington, D. C., 1974.

Rasch, Philip J. An Introduction to the History of Weight Training in the United States. In Sills, Frank, ed., *Weight Training in Sports and Physical Education*. Washington, D. C.: AAHPER, 1962, pp.1-14.

Rasch, Philip J., and Burke, Roger K. *Kinesiology and Applied Anatomy*, 6th ed. Philadelphia: Lea & Febiger, 1978.

Willoughby, David P. *The Super Athletes*. New York: A. S. Barnes and Co., 1970.

Wilmore, Jack H. *Athletic Training and Physical Fitness*. Boston: Allyn and Bacon, Inc., 1976, pp. 67-86.

Appendix 5:
Questions and answers

MULTIPLE CHOICE

1. The greatest prestige is attached to winning
   a. the AAU Mr. America   c. the NABBA Mr. Universe
   b. the IFBB Mr. America   d. the WBBG Mr. America   (p. 70)
2. The lifters at York have popularized
   a. the heavy and light system   c. the set system
   b. the light and heavy system   (p. 34)
3. The use of the squat with heavy weights was popularized by
   a. Mark H. Berry   b. Bob Hoffman   c. Henry J. Atkin   (p. 21)
4. In the opinion of Peary Rader, the most effective system for building up the arms is
   a. sets   b. supersets   c. super multiple sets   (p. 38)
5. The "Valsalva phenomenon" results from
   a. a sudden rise in blood pressure, followed by a sudden drop
   b. a sudden drop in blood pressure, followed by a sudden rise
   c. a sudden and sustained rise in blood pressure   (p. 14)
6. As a rough guide a beginner may start his presses with
   a. one quarter of his body weight   c. one half of his body weight
   b. one third of his body weight   (p. 31)
7. The amount of force that a muscle can exert depends on the number and size of its
   a. sarcoplasm   b. sarcolemma   c. myofibrils   (p. 4)
8. The PHA System is the opposite of the
   a. rest-pause system   c. multipoundage system
   b. blitz system   (p. 36)
9. The present trend in set training is
   a. to use lighter weights in each successive set
   b. to use the same weight in each successive set
   c. to use heavier weights in each successive set   (p. 38)
10. A man who is pressed for time may prefer to use
    a. the multipoundage system   b. a blitz program   c. a split routine   (p. 39)

11. The condition known as "muscle-bound"
    a. does not exist
    b. is commonly found among weight trainers
    c. is found only among men who train incorrectly   (p. 11)
12. Vigorous exercise
    a. will "sweat out" a cold
    b. does not have any effect on its progress
    c. may make it worse   (p. 14)
13. Circuit training is popular with athletes and the military because
    a. it provides cardiorespiratory stress
    b. it provides muscular stress
    c. it is quick and simple   (p. 36)
14. The rest-pause system
    a. is better for the production of strength than of hypertrophy
    b. is better for the production of hypertrophy than of strength
    c. is equally good for either one   (p. 36)
15. The principle use of a swing bell is
    a. to introduce exercises which cannot be done with a barbell
    b. to introduce exercises which cannot be done with a dumbbell
    c. to introduce variety into the program   (p. 55)
16. The Zinovieff or Oxford technique used in rehabilitation work is simply another name
    for the
    a. light and heavy system   c. multipoundage system
    b. heavy and light system   (p. 34)
17. The "good morning" exercise is a variation of the
    a. the front raise   b. the high pull-up   c. straight-legged dead lift   (p. 24)
18. The high pull-up is an excellent exercise for the
    a. trapezius   b. quadriceps   c. spinae erectoris   (p. 18)
19. Many experienced weight lifters consider that the basic exercise for the shoulders is
    a. the curl   c. the press off the back of the neck
    b. the bench press   (p. 27)
20. The forearm supinators and pronators receive excellent exercise from
    a. the flying motion   c. the concentration curl
    b. the Zottman curl   (p. 51)
21. A typical superset combination might consist of
    a. curls and presses   c. squats and dead lifts
    b. supine presses and push-ups   (p. 38)
22. When a hopper is used, the amount of weight that can be employed
    a. is reduced   b. remains the same   c. may be increased   (p. 41)
23. To assist in preventing blacking out
    a. Hyperventilate before a lift
    b. Stay in the squatting position as short a time as possible
    c. Lift the weight slowly and carefully   (p. 14)
24. Anabolic steroids are:
    a. recommended for the use of weight trainers
    b. are both harmless and widely used
    c. may have highly undesirable side effects   (p. 10)
25. Progressive resistance exercise tends
    a. to reduce flexibility   c. to increase flexibility
    b. to have no effect on flexibility   (p. 11)
26. "Overtraining" will
    a. reduce both performance capacity and the ability to resist infections
    b. reduce performance capacity but not the ability to resist infections
    c. reduce the ability to resist infections but not performance capacity   (p. 14)

27. Most of the standardized set of exercises now in general use derive from a book
    written by   (p. 16)
    a. Bob Hoffman   b. Peary Rader   c. Theodor Siebert
28. The exercise program which is based on the theory that muscles should be exercised
    in a large number of different ways is known as
    a. the 1001 exercise system   c. the multipoundage system
    b. the super multiple set system   (p. 31)
29. In order to properly evaluate a program a man should be prepared to stay on it
    a. one month   b. three months   c. six months   (p. 39)
30. Once a certain level of strength is reached, further gains
    a. continue to improve performance   c. hinder performance
    b. do not improve performance   (p. 73)
31. A girl complains of being "flat chested." You might suggest she practice
    a. pull-overs, supine presses, flying motions
    b. half squats, presses, curls
    c. high pull-ups, rowing motion, shoulder shrug   (p. 58)
32. An excellent exercise for the triceps is the
    a. dumbbell swing   b. Hise deltoid exercise   c. dumbbell high pull-up
33. The present public acceptance of weight training is attributable largely to the work of
                                                                           (p. 1)
    a. Mark H. Berry   b. Thomas L. Delorme   c. David P. Willoughby
34. The practice of weight-training produces
    a. little improvement in cardiorespiratory function
    b. moderate improvement in cardiorespiratory function
    c. great improvement in cardiorespiratory function   (p. 11)
35. The light and heavy system seem best fitted for the production of
    a. strength   b. hypertrophy   c. definition   (p. 34)
36. The PHA System appears best adapted for the production of
    a. hypertrophy and definition   c. strength and hypertrophy
    b. strength and definition   (p. 48)
37. The primary object of the dumbbell swing is to develop
    a. the biceps and triceps   c. the spinae erectors and deltoids
    b. the trapezius and latissimus dorsi   (p. 48)
38. The average young woman tends to have calves which are too small. To overcome this
    you might prescribe
    a. bent over lateral raises and supine lateral raises
    b. donkey raises and heel raises
    c. front raises and lateral raises   (p. 58)
39. The program used by judoka training at the Kodokan stresses use of
    a. barbells   b. dumbbells   c. calisthenics   (p. 77)
40. Most individuals can
    a. press less with dumbbells than with barbells
    b. press the same with dumbbells as with barbells
    c. press more with dumbbells than with barbells   (p. 46)
41. The goal in the blitz system is
    a. to keep the blood in constant circulation
    b. to keep the blood in a limited area
    c. to avoid any influence on the blood   (p. 35)
42. A friend asks for an effective exercise for the triceps. You might suggest
    a. bent arm pull-over   c. French press
    b. high pull-up   (p. 30)
43. The correlation between the girth of the forearm and the strength of the handgrip is
    a. low   b. moderate   c. high   (p. 29)

44. It is generally agreed that the average individual requires each night about
    a. seven hours of sleep   c. nine hours of sleep
    b. eight hours of sleep   (p. 6)
45. Jay Silvester, the best combined shot-put and discuss thrower in the world, uses
    a. a light and heavy program   c. a multipoundage program
    b. a heavy and light program   (p. 79)
46. In a normal training routine, the optimal length of rest pauses appears to be about
    a. one minute   b. two minutes   c. three minutes   (p. 6)
47. The front raise with dumbbells is particualrly beneficial to the
    a. deltoids   b. triceps   c. biceps   (p. 47)
48. Normally a man should work out
    a. three times a week   c. fives times a week
    b. four times a week   (p. 31)
49. However, a man on a split routine might train
    a. four days a week   c. six days a week
    b. five days a week   (p. 39)
50. A man doing a reverse curl should expect to handle about
    a. one third as much as he does in the regular curl
    b. one half as much as he does in the regular curl
    c. two thirds as much as he does in the regular curl   (p. 19)
51. The major portion of the diet should be
    a. protein   b. carbohydrate   c. fat   (p. 7)
52. One of your students desires to exercise his abdominus oblique muscles. You might suggest
    a. the dumbbell swing   c. the side bend
    b. the "good morning" exercise   (p. 51)
53. The training program should provide for
    a. short, frequent rest pauses   c. rest pauses whenever fatigue occurs
    b. long, infrequent rest pauses   (p. 6)
54. In performing dead lifts it is best to
    a. have both hands facing forward
    b. have one hand facing forward and one backward
    c. have both hands facing backward   (p. 23)

TRUE OR FALSE

t f   55. The publishers of magazines on weight training have made substantial contributions to our understanding of the physiology of activity.   (p. 18)

t f   56. The AMA Committee on the Medical Aspects of Sports has condemned the half squat as "potentially dangerous to the internal and supporting structures of the knee joint."   (p. 21)

t f   57. Technically, no work is accomplished during isometric exercise, even though the exerciser becomes fatigued.   (p. 3)

t f   58. John Jesse believes that a training program for weight throwers should concentrate on the development of tremendous overall strength.   (p. 79)

t f   59. The AAU disbars any athlete known to have used drugs.   (p. 9)

t f   60. In the PHA system, a sequence consists of five or six exercises arranged in such a way that each affects a different part of the body.   (p. 36)

t f   61. The consumption of large quantities of milk is essential to the weight trainer.   (p. 7-8)

t f   62. The quality of female muscle is the same as that of male muscle.   (p. 56)

t f   63. Muscle girths should be measured before, not after, exercise.   (p. 63)

t f   64. To some extent at least champions are born, not made.   (p. 5)

t f   65. Weight training for women is essentially the same as weight training for men.   (p. 58)

t f   66. The use of tobacco is extremely deleterious to the development of strength and hypertrophy.   (p. 10)
t f   67. Only rarely are body builders outstanding athletes.   (p. 68)
t f   68. The athlete may take it as an axiom that "The more strength and hypertrophy the better."   (p. 73)

COMPLETION

69. Nutritionists recommend that the daily diet be based on the Basic Four Plan. The four are 1. *Milk and milk products; 2. Meat, fish, and eggs; 3. Fruits and vegetables; 4. Breads and cereals.*   (p. 7)
70. The international organization governing physique contests is *(Federation International Halterophile et Culturiste).*   (p. 70)
71. The results of a program of progressive resistance exercise seems to depend upon the following variable [(1) *stress placed on muscles; (2) duration of exercise period; (3) frequency of exercise periods].*   (p. 5)
72. The key question in any discussion of the development of muscle is, *("What can you do with them?")*   (p. 73)
73. One advantage of circuit training is that it may be *("biased")* to give specialized work to certain muscle groups.   (pp. 35-36)
74. Muscular contraction may be divided into the following types, *(isotonic, isometric, lengthening).*   (p. 3)
75. The traditional prescription for losing weight is *(low)* resistance and *(high)* repetitions; for gaining weight it is *(high)* resistance and *(low)* repetitions.   (p. 10)
76. The disadvantage of going on a strict diet is that one may lose *(muscle tone)* as well as weight.   (p. 10)
77. Those who advocate practice of a few heavy exercises for gaining weight emphasize the slogan *(bulk up, train down).*   (p. 11)
78. It has been shown that harm may result from massive doses of vitamin (A, D, M).   (p. 8)
79. Vitamin supplementation may be required in the case of athletes who *(must make weight)* or who *(train very strenuously).*   (p. 8)
80. The bulk craze has caused many body builders to lose sight of the fact that the *(individual measurements must be in proportion).*   (p. 65)
81. Use of the straight-arm lateral raise and the straight-arm pull-over is subject to the objection that *(they may cause deltoid strain or overstretch the elbow joint).*   (pp. 23, 48-49)
82. Few deaths have occurred as a result of weight training. In each case the death was the result of a weight falling on a man during practice of the *(supine press).*   (p. 14)
83. The reducing diet must contain sufficient *(vitamins and minerals)* but be relatively low in *(calories).*   (p. 14)
84. The "overload principle" states that *(strength increases in response to repetitive exercise against progressively increased resistance).*   (pp. 4-5)
85. The dangerous point during dead lifting is the period during which the upper body *(is fully flexed).*   (pp. 23-24)
86. The basic principle of isokinetic exercise is *(to provide resistance proportional to the input of muscular force and alterations in skeletal levers throughout the range of motion).*   (p. 3)
87. The general rule for breathing during weight training is to *(inhale)* while contracting the muscles and *(exhale)* while relaxing them.   (p. 14)
88. Some of the older weight trainers are prejudiced against the use of dumbbells on the grounds *(that they make a man "stiff").*   (p. 46)
89. The purpose of the "cheat" in a cheating exercise is to *(get the weight past the "sticking point").*   (p. 35)

90. One factor which stands out in all studies of weight training is the great individual differences in response to training programs. (p. 33)
91. All advanced training methods depend upon the following principle (increasing the amount of stress placed upon the body within the given training period). (p. 33)
92. The basic principle in the heavy and light system is (to keep working the muscles against near maximal resistance). (p. 34)
93. Some instructors contend that the position assumed in the bent over rowing motion should be avoided because (the long lever and the weight of the upper body and resistance place a great strain on the lower back). (p. 27)
94. In practicing the Zottman curl, the amount of weight that can be handled will be controlled by (the strength that can be exerted in the reverse curl). (p. 51)
95. Too much protein in the diet may leave an (acid residue) which throws an extra load on (the kidneys). (p. 8)
96. The rowing motion to the waist appears to have more effect on the (latissimus dorsi) muscle than does the rowing motion to the chest. (p. 27)
97. In performing POBNs it is essential that the weight not be allowed to (drop on the vertebrae of the neck). (p. 26)
98. It has been said that "More people believe more bunk about (food and nutrition) than any other single topic in the health field." (p. 7)
99. If a muscle is worked regularly the following changes will occur: (a permanent increase in the number of capillaries; the ability of the muscle to assimilate nutritive materials will improve; the size and functional power of the cells will improve). (p. 4)
100. In routine dumbbell training, most trainers seem to prefer (alternate) exercises. (p. 46)

QUESTION ANSWER KEY

Multiple Choice

1. c	12. b	23. b	34. a	45. a
2. a	13. a	24. c	35. a	46. c
3. a	14. a	25. c	36. b	47. a
4. c	15. c	26. a	37. c	48. a
5. a	16. b	27. c	38. b	49. c
6. a	17. c	28. a	39. b	50. c
7. c	18. a	29. c	40. a	51. b
8. b	19. c	30. b	41. b	52. c
9. b	20. b	31. a	42. c	53. a
10. c	21. a	32. b	43. b	54. b
11. c	22. c	33. b	44. b	

True-False

55. F	60. T	65. T
56. F	61. F	66. F
57. T	62. T	67. T
58. F	63. T	68. F
59. T	64. T	

ANSWERS TO EVALUATION QUESTIONS

* No answer

Page   ANSWER AND PAGE REFERENCE

---

7   a. Organically grown food has no more nutritional value than food grown in the usual manner. (p. 7)

    b. Milk is not a dietary essential and may not be tolerated well. (p. 7)

    c. No benefit results from the use of protein supplements or massive doses of vitamins. (p. 8)

    d. There are no miracle foods. (p. 8)

    e. Anabolic steroids are of doubtful value at best and may cause serious side effects. (pp. 9-10)

9   No. The movement should begin with the joint fully extended. Mechanical efficiency is greatest at about 1/5 of the maximal speed. (p. 6)

15   a. Keep weight close to body when lifting. (p. 13)

    b. Don't lift weight from floor when in a stooping position. Correct these faults by stepping close to the object, then bending the knees, keeping the spine as erect as possible. The lift should be done with the legs. (p. 13)

20   *

50   *

54   *

57   *

60   *

66   *

70   *

80   a. The weight training movements should simulate the actual sports movements. (p. 80)

    b. Research needed includes determining the optimum strength level for various forms of activity and the relationships between strength increases and gains in performance. (p. 73)

Name Index

Subject Index

1. White Fiber   quickness (~~buitt~~
2. Red   indurance (build by
                         running)

3. Weight Training   Resistence in an
                              exercise.
              { in W.T. you built streyht,
              { indurance and cardio vascular.

To built white fiber there's
isokenetic (the harder you
push the harder the machine
push.)
concentric (lifting a weight)
excentric (lowering weight)

2 kinds of lift ① Isometric - Means
       pushing immovable object and
② Isotonic (the best way - putting
     your muscle into a full range
     motions
MX (maximum) the most you can lift in
       one lap.
Repitition (the number of lift
set (group of repitition)
Balistic stretch (fast stretch and is
          ~~bad for you~~
Static stretch (slow stretch, your
     muscle get max. stretch)